VENDETTA

The Book on which the HBO Movie is Based!

Antonio D'Alfonso, editor.

Guernica Editions Inc.

P.O. Box 117, Station P, Toronto (ON), Canada M5S 2S6
2250 Military Drive, Tonawanda, N.Y. 14150-6000 U.S.A.
Gazelle, Falcon House, Queen Square, Lancaster LR1 1RN U.K.
Printed in Canada.
Legal Deposit — First Quarter.
National Library of Canada
Library of Congress Card Number: 99-76576
Canadian Cataloguing in Publication Data
Gambino, Richard
Vendetta : the true story of the largest lynching in U.S. history
2nd edition.
(Picas series ; 22)
Includes bibliographical references.
ISBN 1-55071-103-2

1. Mass murder — Louisiana — New Orleans
— History — 19th century.
2. Italian Americans — Louisiana —
New Orleans — History — 19th century.
3. Lynching — Louisiana — New Orleans
— History — 19th century.
I. Title. II. Series.
HV6565.L6G35 1999 364.1'34. C99-901559-1

TO GAIL,
MY WIFE AND HELPMATE,
WITH LOVE

PICAS SERIES 22

Canadä

Guernica Editions acknowledge the financial support of the
Government of Canada through the Book Publishing Industry
Development Program (BPIDP).

RICHARD GAMBINO

VENDETTA

THE TRUE STORY OF THE LARGEST LYNCHING IN U.S. HISTORY

GUERNICA
TORONTO·BUFFALO·LANCASTER (U.K.)
2000

That the hypocrite reign not, lest the people be ensnared.

Job 34:30

Preface

This book tells the story of the slaughter of eleven men by what a grand jury called "several thousand of the first, best and even most law abiding of the citizens" of New Orleans on March 14, 1891. It is the largest lynching in American history.* Every character and event described in these pages is as close to truth as I can determine. All of the dialogue, for example, is taken verbatim from actual newspaper stories and court and other records of the time.

Yet this is more than the story of a bloody mass murder, for it was no "ordinary lynching." The political and economic motives behind the horror are exposed, and the consequences of the drama are laid out. In them one sees the many uses that governments, institutions, and individuals make of social violence, ethnic and racial hatred, propaganda and hypocrisy—and one sees the courage and the peril of the people who oppose such hell. And the story is of more than just historical interest. Although some of the methods of this social violence that are described herein, especially the terror of lynching, are now rare, they are frequently

---

* As measured by the number of people illegally killed in one place at one time, the victims' identities predetermined for some specific alleged offense. "Lynching" here is distinguished, as is usual, from race riots and other forms of civil disorder in which victims are chosen without regard to their individual identities and in which no specific offense on their part is alleged. The 1974 edition of the *Encyclopaedia Britannica* defines lynching as "a form of mob violence in which a mob executes a presumed offender . . . the summary killing of an individual for a real or supposed crime . . ." Lists of lynchings kept by the National Asssociation for the Advancement of Colored People confirm that the lynching described in this book is the largest.

ix

replaced by more refined ways of dividing and controlling people —ways just as effective. The basic social and political patterns one sees in this book still flourish.

In regard to Italian-Americans, the New Orleans lynching was at once both a means of limiting their position, participation, and possibilities in the American community at the time, and one of the first major stimuli of the stereotype of inherently criminal Italian-American culture, a common defamation which still limits the ethnic group's position, participation, and possibilities in today's America.

If it is true that eternal vigilance is the price of liberty, then we had better pay greater attention to certain monstrous traditions of America, as well as observing our real reasons for pride in the bicentennial period in which this book is published. But even if there were not serious lessons to be learned from the events in this book, they would still demand to be told. An injustice which remains hidden, without reparation, never rests. And this is the story of one of the worst, and most covered up, American injustices.

Research for this book was done in New Orleans, Washington, D.C., New York, and Rome. I am indebted to several people for helping me in the work. I wish to thank Major Henry M. Morris, Chief of Detectives of the New Orleans Police Department; Collin B. Hamer, Jr., director of the Louisiana Division of the New Orleans Public Library; the staff of the Louisiana State Museum Library, New Orleans; Commander Richard T. Speer, U. S. Navy, head of the Ships Histories Branch of the Naval Historical Center, Washington, D.C.; Dr. Giuseppe Cardillo, director of the Istituto Italiano di Cultura, New York; and Mimi B. Penchansky of the Queens College Library Interlibrary Department.

Any errors of fact or interpretation which may be in this book, however, are solely my responsibility.

I also wish to thank Walter I. Bradbury, Professor Jean Scarpaci, and Charles Romeo for their assistance; Dr. Joseph S. Murphy, president of Queens College, for his support and encouragement; and my uncle, Santo V. Tranchina, for introducing me to New Orleans.

I offer a special thank-you to my wife, Gail, to whom this book is dedicated, for intelligent criticism and loving support through the bright and dark days of research and writing.

1

New Orleans is a damp city, and the mud in the unpaved streets of the Old French Quarter was topped by an inch of water the night of October 15, 1890. It had rained so hard earlier in the evening that men took off their shoes and rolled their pants above their knees to cross the streets between wooden sidewalks. Now the rain had stopped, but a warm, drizzly mist hung in the air. Holding an umbrella overhead, the city's Police Superintendent, David C. Hennessy, suggested to his friend Bill O'Connor that they walk up Rampart Street. "The sidewalks on Basin Street are very bad," he explained.

At age thirty-two, Hennessy was one of the youngest police chiefs in the country. He was also the most famous. Newspapers across the nation had been headlining his exploits for several years ever since he was a very young detective. Rawboned and muscular, he had a reputation as fearless, smart, and aggressive. "Stalwart" was the press's favorite word to describe him. He thoroughly enjoyed the distinction. He also enjoyed the friendship of powerful people in Louisiana and beyond, people like Chicago's William A. Pinkerton, of the famous private police agency, which, in a tirne of ineffective municipal departments and no FBI, had grown to a national police force. Bill O'Connor, a former city policeman, was a captain in another of the armed private forces, the Boylan Protective Police. The Boylan force patrolled New Orleans' streets and generally rivaled the city's Police Department in authority and power.

Hennessy had spent the evening at a meeting of the city's Police Board at the old City Hall. Afterward, he went to his office in the Central Police Station, then located at South Basin and Common streets. O'Connor stopped by at about 10 P.M. and decided that he would accompany the Chief home. Hennessy, a bachelor, worked late most nights and always walked the few blocks to his home. Later, others of Hennessy's friends said they sometimes accompanied him home because his life had been threatened, but particulars about the threat were never revealed.

An uncharacteristic quiet hung over the French Quarter as the two policemen walked through the mist. The Chief suggested to O'Connor that they stop at one of his favorite places, Dominic Virget's Oyster Saloon at Rampart and Poydras streets, to have a late snack. Each man ate a half dozen oysters, and Hennessy, a teetotaler in a hard-drinking town, washed his down with a glass of milk.

As O'Connor later told reporters, the Chief was relaxed and in a good mood. He recalled that their conversation that night was the ordinary talk of old friends. After the small meal, they continued at a leisurely pace along Rampart Street.

When they got to the corner of Girod Street, they paused a moment to finish a sentence or two. Then Hennessy said, according to O'Connor, "There's no need to come any further with me now, Bill. You go on your own way." The two men shook hands, and O'Connor splashed across the street and walked toward the Mississippi River. Hennessy remained on the north side and walked in the opposite direction, toward his home at 275 Girod Street, midway between Basin and Franklin streets. In 1890, the neighborhood was a greatly dilapidated area of small cottages, rooming houses, and shanties housing many poor people, including blacks and immigrant Italians. Hennessy lived alone with his mother, who had grown attached to the neighborhood over many years. In deference to her wishes, they continued to live there long after her son had attained position and fame.

Hennessy had covered about three quarters of the block to Basin Street when five men appeared directly across the street. There was a great explosion heard for blocks as they opened fire with shotguns, and perhaps also with rifles or pistols. It happened so fast that the Chief, a man noted for his quickness, didn't have a

2

chance to turn. A dense cloud of speeding lead slammed into his left side. Slugs and pellets shredded his umbrella and tore into the sidewalk all around him and into the cottage at 269 Girod Street, in front of which he was walking. Two small children and their mother were terrified, but unharmed, as several shots smashed into their bedrooms in the house. Witnesses later said they heard from six to as many as eighteen or twenty blasts and shots fired.

Hennessy screamed in pain as the fusillade knocked him sideways against the cottage. Three heavy slugs had ripped into his abdominal area, tearing his stomach and intestines. One entered his chest, piercing the membrane around the heart; a fifth smashed his left elbow; a sixth broke his right leg; and his torso as well as both arms and both legs had been chewed by shotgun pellets.

The ambush was over in seconds. The assailants broke and ran west toward Basin Street.

Hennessy now proved his legendary toughness. He drew his pistol and began to run after the gunmen. As they approached the corner of Basin Street across the street from him, Hennessy fired two shots at them through the dense gun smoke, both of which were later dug out of a two-story frame house behind the fleeing gunmen. The location of the bullets showed that the Chief's aim was still close to level despite his terrible wounds. The wounded man then tripped upon the steps of a secondhand-goods store. By the time he pulled himself to his feet, three of the gunmen were running in the next block of Girod Street, passing Hennessy's home. Two others had turned south on Basin Street. Hennessy stumbled about six or seven feet to Basin and fired another shot. He then staggered northward on Basin and collapsed in front of a frame house at number 189, between Girod and Lafayette streets. As he fell, he shouted, "Billy, Billy!"

Bill O'Connor remembered that he had passed two policemen on patrol as he walked on Girod Street. He had just reached the corner at Dryades Street when he heard the first gunfire. He whirled about toward Basin Street, two blocks away. He saw gun flashes and heard more shots. Running toward them, he quickly came upon a Boylan cop. "Which way did they run?" shouted

O'Connor. "I think it was uptown," the patrolman yelled back. They ran to Basin Street, just in time to hear Hennessy shout, "Billy, Billy!" As they got to him, they were joined by a city policeman and another Boylan officer. These two officers were holding a Negro whom they said they "found running at full speed."

"They gave it to me," Hennessy said to the cops, "and I gave them back the best I could." Later that night, O'Connor told reporters, "Bending over the Chief I said to him: 'Who gave it to you, Dave?' He replied, 'Put your ear down here.' As I bent down again, he whispered the word 'Dagoes.'" No one but O'Connor heard Hennessy's whispered reply.

O'Connor hurried to a nearby grocery store and telephoned for an ambulance. He then telephoned the Mayor and the Police Commissioner. It was midnight.

By morning word had flashed throughout the nation and to Europe of the attack upon America's foremost expert on the Sicilian "stiletto" and "vendetta" societies, as they were called. Millions of people on both sides of the Atlantic were stunned by reports that the famous Dave Hennessy had been cut down by the dreaded and mysterious "Mafia," a name recently introduced to Americans.

The guns on Girod Street roared a beginning to a series of bloody and dark events that were soon to embroil officials in New Orleans, Rome, and Washington, including the President of the United States. The consequences were enormous. The events helped erase all of the rights and power achieved by Louisiana's black people after the Civil War. They were to set the embryonic labor movement back in New Orleans. They contributed to America's closing the gates of immigration against the "scum of Europe." The events were used to create a scare of war with a European power that helped unite the country behind a military lobby which built America's "New Navy," the navy that launched the United States on its career as a global power eight years later in the Spanish-American War. And the events so poisoned the country's relations with Italian-Americans that when President

4

Benjamin Harrison denounced their mass murder in New Orleans as "an offense against law and humanity," there was talk in Congress of impeaching him. Yet, until now, these incredible events have never been fully revealed.

2

Mayor Joseph A. Shakspeare led several dozen people who kept watch with Hennessy during the long night at old Charity Hospital, then housed in a large whitewashed building constructed in 1832. Ironically, a substantial part of the hospital's revenue at the time came from a tax imposed on the people who were to be accused of Hennessy's murder. The tax was levied on immigrants landing in New Orleans through the captains of immigrant ships. And, since 1880, most of the large number of immigrants to the city had been Italians from Sicily.

Hennessy had been treated by a special medical team on entering the hospital. When he saw them, the wounded man greeted them with "Doctors, how are you?" and tried to take off his jacket for them. After replying that they were fine, and restraining the Chief, the doctors dressed his wounds, which they pronounced "very dangerous but not necessarily fatal."

The Police Chief was given enough opiates to ease his pain, but not enough to knock him out. He was to remain fully conscious during most of the night, and his mind was clear and calm, as is evident in the accounts of his conversations. At about one o'clock in the morning, he received last rites from a Catholic priest. He talked with the priest for a few minutes, then asked a friend for a glass of milk. The man answered that it was against the doctors' orders because of his stomach wounds. "Are those the orders?" asked Hennessy. His friend nodded. "Then I won't ask any more." The Chief was given some cracked ice to relieve his thirst. He was asked if he had a statement to make, and he answered, "I'm all right. I'm not going to die. I'm going to get over this."

Hennessy's widowed mother soon arrived. She had raised her

only child by herself since he was a nine-year-old boy. When he saw her, Hennessy said, "Mother, why did you come? Don't worry yourself. Go home, and I'll be with you soon. I'm all right." The other visitors quietly advised the woman to remain, and she stayed.

Again the Chief was asked if he had anything to say. His answer, heard by several people, was, "Your alarm is unnecessary. Those people can't kill me." No one thought to ask him who "those people" were.

Hennessy's mother was sent to wait at home, not far away. Upon her leaving, a judge of the City Recorder's Court stepped into a circle of people around Hennessy's bed. "Chief," he said, "your mother has just left the room. You know who I am and my capacity. Do you wish to make a declaration?" He answered, "No, I don't think I'm that bad off." The judge stayed close by. Still later in the night, Hennessy was asked again if he had anything to say and, again, the reply was negative.

During these hours, Bill O'Connor repeated his story about Hennessy saying "dagoes" shot him to crowds of people in the corridor outside Hennessy's room, including reporters and city officials.

In the same corridor, Mayor Shakspeare, in the presence of the entire crowd, gave orders to the police: "Scour the whole neighborhood! Arrest every Italian you come across, if necessary, and scour it again tomorrow morning as soon as there is daylight enough. Get all the men you need." The police complied, and almost every city policeman was ordered into the case, joined by the entire Boylan force.

At about 9 A.M., Hennessy had been lying quietly for a few minutes, when suddenly his eyelids and nostrils twitched. A doctor pushed his way through the crowd, examined him, and at 9:06, more than nine hours after the shooting, pronounced him dead. Although it was well known that Hennessy knew by sight virtually every Italian criminal in New Orleans, and knew all of the prominent Italians in the city personally, no one had asked him directly if he could name any of his assailants—or if they were in fact Italians.

At the moment of Hennessy's death, some fifty Italians had already been arrested, and between one and two hundred more were to be taken during the next twenty-four hours.

The morning issue of the New Orleans *Times-Democrat* was already on the streets when Hennessy died. It carried an ominous large advertisement calling upon the city's people to form "committees . . . to assist the officers of the law in driving the murderous Mafia from our midst" and urging the City Council to give its blessing to the vigilante groups.

It was not until four months later that anyone prominent in New Orleans raised a certain basic question. On February 16, 1891, an anonymous writer for the New Orleans *New Delta,* in a column buried way down on page 2, made a passing observation. "The wonder now," he wrote, "is that the sole grounds for the wholesale arrest of the Italians were the single word, 'Dagoes,' uttered by the wounded man to his friend Captain O'Connor. For nine hours Mr. Hennessy survived his injuries, and during that time he was able to converse with his friends. The public . . . cannot help expressing a surprise that no questions were put to the wounded man, so that the great mystery might have been elucidated."

3

By the time David C. Hennessy died on the morning of October 16, 1890, the city of New Orleans and its newspapers were awash in wild stories and rumors about his killing. Captain O'Connor was not the only policeman talking liberally to the press about the "dagoes" who killed the Chief. The murder area had been thick with city and private policemen at the time of the shooting. A private watchman at a nearby lumberyard excitedly told reporters, "I was walking on Julia Street when I met three men. That was after I had heard the shooting. 'What was the shooting?' I asked. 'Me no know,' was the reply of a dago. The three were dagoes. I passed on, and right behind the first were two more men. One of them had a short gun, which he seemed to be trying to hide under his coat. I had no reason to stop them and they got past me. Then I turned around and they began running. Three ran out Julia into the lumber yard, and two of them ran down Liberty. The fellow with the rifle was a tall man with a derby hat. The others had on slouch hats. I could not see their faces, it was so dark. They had on dark clothes." A reporter for the *Daily Picayune* added that "no further traces of the men were discovered."

Another private policeman told newsmen, "I was on Rampart and Girod Street when the shooting took place. It was dark. The lights [the electric streetlights] were almost out, but went up just as they fired. I ran down there. Two ran up Franklin Street, and one ran out Girod Street toward the woods. They all disappeared in the darkness, and so suddenly we thought they had gone into houses around here. Two of the men had guns and one had a pistol."

Three officers claimed to have chased the murderers together.

"I ran after them," one said, "and would have fired at them, only a boy was in the way and I didn't want to hurt an innocent man. Two ran up Franklin and one out Girod Street. One was about 5 feet 9½ inches high and had on a light coat and dark pants. The other two were about 5 feet 6 inches. Both were rather stout; one wore a dark striped suit, and the other a dark suit. They wore slouch hats, and the tall man a derby. We were about 75 feet behind them when they disappeared. The lights were out all around."

The papers reported that an "Officer Cotton of Boylan's police" had been grazed on the head by a shot fired by Chief Hennessy. They also reported that another Boylan cop, "Officer J. C. Roe," had been "shot in the ear." Unless they were directly involved in the gunfire that killed Hennessy or his return shots, it is difficult to explain the wounds of these two policemen. All references to their wounds soon disappeared from the accounts of the murder night.

Several other facts emerge about these on-the-spot policemen. First, none claimed to have seen the faces of the gunmen. Second, most of them described the killers as Italians. And most peculiar of all, only two of the ten policemen who claimed to see Hennessy's killers were later called upon to testify at the trial of those accused of the murder. Among those *not* called was Bill O'Connor, with whom entirely rested the claim that "dagoes" killed the Chief.

Another fact left unexplained was that reporters noted that, in addition to many bullet and shot marks at the scene where Hennessy was ambushed, "houses *on the next block,* between Franklin and Basin, showed bullet marks." In particular, Chief Hennessy's house on this street "bore the marks of no less than fifteen or eighteen bullets and small shot, all of which had struck in a slanting direction from the direction of Basin Street." Evidently, someone had done a lot of shooting at Hennessy's house, more than half a block from where he was killed.

In addition to the policemen, other witnesses to Hennessy's shooting came forward. When questioned the next morning at his place of employment, Mr. F. Peeler, who lived on the second floor of the building on Girod and Basin streets next to where the gun-men stood when they shot at Hennessy, said he jumped to his win-dow when he heard the first shots. He saw a "short, thick set man who wore an oil cloth coat" firing from a kneeling position in the middle of the street, and two others firing from the sidewalk. He shouted at them to stop, and the three then ran off in a "stooping position."

The building in front of which the gunmen stood had an alley on its west side and a yard with a wide unlocked gate on its east side. The yard extended behind the building, so that the entire structure was surrounded by empty space. There was a shanty in front of the two-story house. A forty-two-year-old Italian shoe repairman named Pietro Monasterio lived in the shed's front room. For years, this room had been rented by newly arrived Ital-ian immigrants as a residence, sometimes also as a fruit stand. After living in it a few weeks, the new arrival would move to per-manent quarters. Monasterio had lived there for two months.

In two rooms behind Monasterio's, with an entrance on the alley, lived a black teamster named John Beverly and his wife. Beverly told police that Monasterio often had many "visitors," all Italians—who may have been customers of the cobbler. Early in the evening of October 15, Beverly said, an Italian called on Monasterio, and the two men had "a long, whispered conver-sation" in Italian. The Beverlys went to bed at nine o'clock. When they were awakened by the gun blasts outside their shed, Mrs. Beverly said, "There's that dago, shooting at some one around his place." They heard someone, probably Hennessy, cry out in pain, and the woman pleaded with Beverly not to go out. The couple said that neither one of them went to a window or door for a few moments for fear of being shot. Then Beverly went out to the front of the building, followed by a neighbor named Emma Thomas. There they saw Monasterio before his open door, "standing in his underclothes." He turned to them and shouted excitedly, "Emma, Emma! The Chief, the Chief, mamma's shoes!" Mrs. Thomas understood that Monasterio, who spoke very little English, was trying to tell her that someone had been shot and it

11

was Hennessy, whom he recognized because he had once repaired the Chief's mother's shoes.

Another black woman, Mary Rose Wheeler, who lived on the same street, said she went to her window after the shots and saw "men running," and that "one had a gun in his hand."

All these witnesses said they had *not* seen the gunmen's faces.

While the on-the-spot policemen and the civilian witnesses told their inconclusive stories as the Chief lay dying, Mayor Shakspeare was making it clear that he had no doubts about who had shot him. He told reporters, "Things have come to a pretty pass when the heads of government in America are in danger of their lives." He then followed up his previous order to "arrest every Italian" by instructing the police to place "an officer on every corner of every Italian neighborhood" and "report the coming and going of every Italian." The Acting Police Chief answered that his men were "at work examining all of the luggers [small fishing boats] and the resorts of the lower class of Sicilians along the riverfront and none of the latter will be able to leave the city unobserved, and any of them who cannot give a straight account of themselves for the past twenty-four hours will be promptly arrested."

The police complied by arresting Italians en masse. A typical incident was described by the New York *Times*. The police stormed into an Italian saloon on the corner of Conti and Burgundy streets and arrested all thirty Italian men who were present. "The police," the paper said, "hustled them to jail with considerable rude treatment, but the principal fact against them was that they could not speak English." Within the next week the Consul of the Italian Government in New Orleans sent a letter to Mayor Shakspeare and personally visited the Governor and Attorney General of Louisiana to complain of the mass arrests and beatings of Italians and of the rough searches of their homes. He also complained that Italian boys as young as twelve years old had been arrested, and asked that the Italians in jail "be treated with the same consideration as those of other nationalities."

Within three hours of Hennessy's death, five of the dozens of

Italians questioned and arrested were charged by the police "for the willful murder of David C. Hennessy." The shoddy police work that led to their arrest and being charged set the stage for what was to follow—a persecution of Italians rather than a true investigation of the murder.

Sergeant McCabe of the city police had arrived on the ambush scene when Hennessy was still lying where he had collapsed. When morning broke he "began to search for some of the dagoes" —whose identities were unknown. When he learned that a forty-four-year-old Italian named Antonio Bagnetto was away from his fruit stand in the Poydras Market, he found it "strange" and went looking for him. He found the man walking on Rampart Street. He searched him, found a fully loaded six-shot revolver in his pocket—not unusual in New Orleans, where thousands of men and women carried guns—and arrested him. McCabe told reporters that Bagnetto said to him, "Do you want to be a friend of mine? Take this pistol and keep it for yourself and you will make as good a friend of mine as a brother, and plenty of Italian friends. If you don't do that, you know what will happen." Before finding Bagnetto, McCabe had discovered another fully loaded revolver lying in the mud on Rampart Street. Some newspapers misreported that Bagnetto was also carrying this second pistol.

Later McCabe went in search of another Italian fruit peddler named Antonio Scaffidi, because he was known to wear an oilcloth as a raincoat, as one of the gunmen had been described as wearing. The twenty-four-year-old Scaffidi was employed by an uncle at a fruit stand, also in the Poydras Market. McCabe found his suspect there, reading a newspaper account of Hennessy's shooting. The uncle told the sergeant that Scaffidi had left the stand at 10:30 P.M. wearing an oilcloth. He later returned, still wearing the garment, which the uncle gave to McCabe. McCabe promptly arrested Scaffidi at 9:20 A.M., just fourteen minutes after Hennessy died.

Monasterio, the cobbler, was arrested because he lived in the shack across the street from where Hennessy was shot. The *Daily Picayune* explained that he didn't speak English "and there was

13

nobody around to take his explanation in Italian" when he was arrested in his shed a few minutes after Hennessy's shooting, also by Sergeant McCabe.

Another fruit peddler, forty-four-year-old Antonio Marchesi, was arrested because he was a friend of Monasterio and "was known to frequent his shoe shop." The police also arrested Marchesi's fourteen-year-old son, Gaspare. They brought the boy from Poydras Market to Monasterio's shop. According to the *New Delta,* he was crying and repeating, "I no know nothing." In the shed, he was questioned about Hennessy's shooting and reportedly answered all questions with "No understand English; aska me in Italiano."

A man named Bastian Incardona was arrested at 7:30 A.M. on the corner of Poydras and Dryades streets by a policeman because "he looked suspicious." Wanted in Italy as a petty criminal, he was the only one of the five who had a criminal record.

Of all the dozens, perhaps hundreds of Italians being held on the morning of October 16, these five were formally charged for the following reasons. Three were picked by witnesses—in a very casual and highly dubious way. First, witness F. Peeler was brought to the Central Police Station. Every cell in the building, as well as the captains' and sergeants' lounges, which had been pressed into service as lockups, was jammed full of Italian men. Peeler was taken from cell to cell. Despite his previous statements to reporters that he had not seen the gunmen's faces, he pointed first to Antonio Scaffidi in one cell as the man he had seen wearing the oilcloth coat, kneeling and firing. Before another crowded cell, he selected Incardona as another of the gunmen. In an opposite cell, Peeler pointed to Bagnetto, who was questioned on the spot. Through a translator, he said he had been in New Orleans only a few weeks and that he lived over "Tony Mantranga's oyster saloon," being promised work by Mantranga the following week on one of the city's many ships which brought fruit from Central America. The police considered this association with Mantranga damning, for reasons that will emerge later. Bagnetto was told to

14

put on his coat—a checkered one. Peeler then said he recognized the man better because he had seen the coat.

Mary Wheeler was also given a tour of the cells and rooms. She could not identify any of the prisoners, but "from his size" she said she thought Scaffidi was the man who wore the oilcloth and carried a gun, although she said she had not seen his face.

The lumberyard watchman also looked over the prisoners. Despite his earlier statement that it had been too dark to see faces, he said he thought two or three looked familiar "but was not quite positive" about it.

Monasterio was charged because police theorized that he had housed the gunmen as they lay in wait for Hennessy. They maintained this allegation despite the fact that all the physical evidence discovered was found in the alley, yard, and streets outside the Italian's shed, and nothing of any suspicious nature had been found in his room, except some lines scratched on a wall, in the manner often used to keep track of something's being counted. Police later said Monasterio was counting Hennessy's walks past the shed.

Antonio Marchesi and his son were booked solely because of their known association with Monasterio—a witness said he saw them there earlier in the evening.

During the murder night and the next morning, the police and others found a number of weapons in the streets near the murder scene. Under normal circumstances, these would be useless as evidence because, as a reporter wrote, all night and morning "a great crowd surged up and down the fatal ground." Anyone in the crowd could have dropped the guns.

Three shotguns were found on Julia Street, near Basin. One was of an old-fashioned muzzle-loading type, which the police said was a "favorite" of Italians, despite the fact that muzzle-loading shotguns and rifles were widely in use in New Orleans (and the rest of the South) at the time. (In fact, in museums several can still be seen that had been used a few years before in the battle between a large "citizen army" and the old Metropolitan Police for control of the police in New Orleans, a fight that became known as the "battle of Liberty Place.") A ramrod which could have been used in loading this weapon was found in the alley next to Monasterio's shack.

One of the guns had a hinged stock which permitted it to be folded into a compact "carrying" size. The newspapers of the city said this was a novelty in New Orleans. Although the gun was manufactured by the W. Richards Company, some newspapers in the city mistakenly reported it was of Italian make.

Another muzzle-loader and a more modern breech-loading shotgun were found on Franklin Street near Julia by Sergeant McCabe. Two or three of the shotguns had been crudely sawed down to a short length. Three of the five shotguns were double-barreled weapons. Curiously, each had one barrel discharged and one still loaded. These weapons and Hennessy's pistol alone could not have accounted for the large number of gun reports heard by most witnesses. Although some said they heard seven or eight shots, most said they heard twelve or more. Some claimed hearing eighteen or twenty, an interesting account if related to the unexplained gunshot holes reported in the façade of Hennessy's house a half block from the ambush site.

The police also confiscated a large horse pistol from a gun store on Rampart and Perdido streets simply because it had been brought in the night before, to be repaired, by an Italian. Several other firearms were confiscated from the homes and shops of Italians, and their owners were arrested, despite the fact that they had broken no law and that probably a majority of the men in the city owned guns. No pistols or rifles were found at or near the murder scene, making it hard to account for the large slugs which deeply penetrated Hennessy's body, unless they were fired as shot from the older "musket"-type shotguns. But it is unlikely that the coroner would mistake shotgun loads for pistol bullets. Hennessy was no doubt wounded by pistols as well as shotguns.

After Hennessy died, a large angry crowd formed outside the Central Police Station. It grew larger and more unruly as the morning progressed. When a number of wives and other female relatives of the many Italians being held tried to get to the building, they were pushed around, struck, and driven away by the crowd.

A lawyer who happened to have business that morning in a court in the same building urged the court's judges to stay on hand "to act as a conservator of the peace in the event that citizens might give vent to their feelings regarding the cowardly assassination." Two judges agreed to remain to abort any possible mob action. The five Italians were then booked in this court and held without bail.

At 1:30 P.M., a box-like, mule-drawn "black maria" van arrived at the Central Police Station to take the five booked Italians to the New Orleans Parish Prison. (In Louisiana, counties are called "parishes.") The "immense crowd was kept at bay" by a squad of police, who with the two judges walked alongside the van to the prison "to guard the prisoners from any threatened harm." The crowd also accompanied the van, first shouting obscenities, then taking up the mocking chant: "Who killa de Chief?" At Parish Prison, the prisoners were turned over to Criminal Sheriff Gabriel Villere and the prison warden, Captain Lemuel Davis, who ordered a large squad of guards armed with rifles and shotguns to stand ready in the prison courtyard in case of any mob assault on the building.

A forty-one-year-old black laborer named Zachary Foster was kept prisoner as a "material witness" to the killing, with bail fixed at an impossible-to-meet ten thousand dollars. Evidently he was the Negro captured running from the scene just after Chief Hennessy's ambush. Although he was thoroughly questioned, the otherwise talkative police disclosed nothing to the press or public of what he said. Foster was also taken, separately, to Parish Prison.

Meanwhile, the police continued with hundreds of raids upon Italian homes and shops, and the wholesale arrest of Italians was accelerated.

Mayor Shakspeare didn't like Italians. Eight months after Hennessey's killing, he gave his opinion of them in a letter to a man in Athens, Ohio. The Ohio man had written that the good people of Athens hadn't had any experience with this ethnic group, this "race," to use the term of the day. Since New Orleans had a large number of Italy's children, would the Mayor share his views of them?

The man in Ohio must have been startled by the hatred in the Mayor's reply, brutal even for that period of openly expressed bigotries. On June 9, 1891, Shakspeare instructed his secretary to send a letter giving full expression to his feelings.

> Our genial climate, the ease with which the necessaries of life can be obtained and the polyglot nature of the population unfortunately has singled this part of the country [southern Louisiana] for the idle and the emigrants from the worst classes of Europe, Southern Italians and Sicilians. New Orleans has an unusually large proportion of the immigrants from these countries [sic] and we find them the most idle, vicious and worthless people among us. A very large percentage are fugitives from justice or ex-convicts aided in their emigration by their governments or the communities which seek relief by their departure. They rarely acquire homes, always band together, do not acquire our language and have neither respect for its government [sic] or obedience to its laws. They monopolize the fruit, oyster and fish trades and are nearly all peddlers, tinkers or cobblers (the two last trades are the ones taught in their prisons at home). They are filthy in their persons and homes and our epidemics nearly always break out in their quarter. They are without courage, honor, truth, pride, religion or any quality that goes to make the good citizen.

New Orleans could afford (if such a thing were lawful) to pay for their deportation. Except the Poles we know of no other nationality which is [as] objectional as a people. [The full text of this letter is given in Appendix A.]

Shakspeare certainly wasn't restraining his anti-Italian emotions in the days after Hennessy's killing. He denounced the "race" in emotional terms and claimed that Italians would next attempt to kill him. "I have been elected by thousands of citizens to enforce the law," Shakspeare told the City Council on October 18, "and cannot be deterred from doing my full duty by a band of assassins. No matter what further threats might come, I will go down fighting in the front ranks in the battle to bring to justice the foul murderers of Chief Hennessy." According to the New York *Times,* these words were met with "tremendous applause." Even a historian who admired Shakspeare, John S. Kendall, had to question the Mayor's claim that his life had been threatened. "He did not give the source of his information," said Kendall years later, "which may be set down to rumor and the excitement of the moment, for there was clearly no foundation to it." In 1890, however, Shakspeare was believed, and his "defiant" words brought anti-Italian feelings closer to the boiling point.

Meanwhile, the two officials responsible for Parish Prison, Sheriff Villere and Warden Davis, strengthened the armed guard against possible mob action at the two entrances to the prison, and announced it would be maintained twenty-four hours a day until further notice.

The mood of hatred, then, was thick when the Mayor got to the heart of things before the City Council. The council room was jammed with reporters from around the country. Shakspeare glared around the room at the gathering and the applause instantly gave way to silence. In a low voice, he began to read a prepared statement, starting with the "official announcement" of Hennessy's death. When he came to the main part of his speech, his voice rose to a shrill scream. Having no more evidence than has been described so far in this book, he told the Council that "the circumstances of the cowardly deed, the arrests made and the evidence collected by the police department, show beyond doubt that he was the victim of Sicilian vengeance, wreaked upon him as the chief representative of the law and order in this community because he was seeking, by the power of our American law, to break up the fierce vendettas that have so often stained our streets with blood. Heretofore," he went on, "these scoundrels have confined their murderings among themselves. . . . Bold, indeed, was the stroke aimed at their first American victim. A shining mark have they selected on which to write with the assassin's hand their contempt for the civilization of the new world." (The full text of this statement is in Appendix B.) As he continued, the eighteen councilmen present squirmed in their seats with anger. Several of them were red in the face by the time the Mayor shouted, "We owe it to ourselves and to everything we hold sacred in this life to see to it that this blow is the last. We must teach these people a lesson that they will not forget for all time."

The Council burst into applause. It was ready to give Shakspeare what he wanted. It unanimously passed a resolution authorizing him to appoint a committee of citizens "whose duty it shall be," in the words of the Council's resolution, "to thoroughly investigate the matter of the existence of secret societies or bands of oath-bound assassins, which it is openly charged have life in our midst and have culminated in the assassination of the highest executive officer of the police department, and to devise necessary means and the most effective and speedy measures for the uprooting and total annihilation of such hell-born associations; and also to suggest needful remedies to prevent the introduction here of criminals or paupers from Europe."

The Mayor immediately appointed the members of the group, which, although it numbered eighty-three, became known as the Committee of Fifty. (A full list of Committee members is in Appendix C.) The membership of the Committee represented the political and labor powers, the wealthy commercial establishment, and the social elite of the city. There were, of course, no Italians on it, and no blacks.

Shakspeare appointed Edgar H. Farrar, a powerful attorney, and a member of Tulane University's first Board of Trustees, as Committee chairman, and instructed another lawyer, William S. Parkerson, to act as liaison between him and the Committee. Parkerson, a young man with aristocratic airs, had managed the Mayor's last election campaign and was Shakspeare's quiet agent in most political matters. Although nominally not a member of the Committee, he played a leading role in its activities.

The Council voted a first appropriation of $15,000 to the Committee for its expenses.

Deciding to hold its meeting in absolute secrecy, the Committee of Fifty went right to work, renting fourth-floor offices in the Cotton Exchange Building and calling witnesses to appear before it. It "ordered" all newspaper reporters, as well as all other citizens, not to talk with anyone connected with the case, a command that could not be enforced. On the other hand, Sheriff Villere ordered that no news reporters be permitted to talk to the Italian prisoners in Parish Prison, an order which could be, and was, enforced.

On October 23, the newspapers of New Orleans printed an open letter from the Committee, addressed to the Italian-Americans of New Orleans and signed by the Committee's chairman, Edgar H. Farrar, a remarkable act by the man who was later to become president of the American Bar Association. It began with an announcement that "the committee . . . has concluded for the present to act strictly within the limits of the law," and went on with an invitation to Italian-Americans to betray one another. Any sort of hearsay was fine, even anonymously communicated. "Send us the names and history (so far as you know it) of every bad man, every criminal, and every suspected person of your race in this city or the vicinity. . . . In giving this information, you may reveal your identity or not, just as you please." The letter ended with a sharp threat of violence against all thirty thousand Italian-Americans in and around New Orleans.

We hope this appeal will be met by you in the same spirit in which we issue it, and that this community will not be driven to harsh and stringent methods outside of the law, which may involve the innocent and guilty alike. We believe this committee speaks the unanimous sentiment of the good people of New-Orleans when it declares that vendettas must cease and assassinations must stop. To this we intend to put an end, peaceably and lawfully if we can, violently and summarily if we must. Upon you and your willingness to give information depends which of these courses shall be pursued. [The full text of the Committee's letter is in Appendix D.]

5

Hennessy's funeral was the grandest ever in the history of a city famous for lavish last ceremonies, outshining even the elaborate New Orleans funeral two years earlier of the former President of the Confederate States of America, Jefferson Davis. It was part of a great effort to elevate Hennessy into martyrdom and create a complete "amnesia" about the shadowy circumstances of his death and the darker facets of his life.

Upon his death, Hennessy's body was taken to an undertaker who dressed the corpse in a black suit and, on Shakspeare's orders, placed it in the best coffin in the city, made of the finest mahogany, with silver handles and mountings, and lined with snow-white silk. By noon the coffin was in the parlor of Hennessy's home on Girod Street, guarded by a squad of police. The dead man's face was illuminated through a glass window under the raised lid of the casket by an "immense silver candelabra." According to the New Orleans *Times-Democrat,* the corpse showed "but little sign of decomposition." The candlelight playing on Hennessy's hair, which was heavily streaked with gray, heightened his paleness. The effect was that the late Chief's appearance was "unworldly," even "saintly."

By early afternoon, twenty-five people per minute were marching through the room, every inch of which was packed with ornate floral arrangements. They included a seven-foot representation of the official symbol of New Orleans, an inverted crescent over a five-pointed star. Another piece was in the form of a white dove nestled on a slightly smaller crescent, sent by the Boylan police. Another prominent arrangement was a large lyre of white flowers from William S. Parkerson.

The scene continued late into the night, when the police yielded to Mrs. Hennessy's complaints about the noise of the crowd and closed the house to the public. On the following morning the casket was taken to City Hall for viewing in the Council Chamber, where Jefferson Davis' body had lain. Hennessy's casket was carried all the way from his house to City Hall on the shoulders of police officers. Because of the coffin's heavy weight, the puffing pallbearers had to be changed every three hundred feet or so. The coffin was finally placed on heavy pedestals which rested on a jet-black bearskin rug. A police hat, club, and belt were placed on its lid and its window opened to display Hennessy's face. People filed through the room in even greater numbers than the day before.

They included a group of Chinese children from a mission school, led by a white female teacher. Presumably they were the offspring of some two thousand Chinese laborers who were brought to work in Louisiana's sugar fields in the early 1870s. "They showed the civilizing influences of Christianity," wrote the *Times-Democrat,* and "were dressed in conventional American style, and brought a large basket of flowers as a tribute. The card on the basket said: 'In Grateful Memory of Our Friend.'"

At 2:15 P.M., the police closed the doors to the room as three police captains and Hennessy's black driver stood before the bier. Their prayer was interrupted by a commotion outside. The entire membership of Fire Company Hope No. 3 had arrived late and was clamoring to be let in.

A funeral procession formed for the trip to St. Joseph's Catholic Church, where Mass was said by five Irish-American priests. The procession then went out to suburban Metairie Cemetery. *It was more than a mile long.*

Metairie is the most elegant of New Orleans' historic cemeteries. Because of the moist, marshy soil conditions of the region, all the dead were placed in tombs aboveground in these peculiar cemeteries, which today are a tourist attraction, Metairie having the best marble and granite tombs of all. At 5:33 P.M., Hennessy's casket was pushed halfway into one of the vaults. Then dozens of police filed past it, each man throwing his badge into the opening. A priest spoke a Latin prayer; upon the words "may his soul and those of the faithful departed, in the name of God, rest in peace, amen," the casket was pushed all the way into the vault and the door to the tomb was closed.

Hennessy's transformation into a saintly hero was well underway. In the investigations and discussions of the next months, certain facts about him were completely ignored. They form a good part of his life's record, and cast him in quite a different light than the heroic aura that was placed around him after his death and has remained there ever since.

6

To say David C. Hennessy lived with violence all his life would be a great understatement.

His father leaped into the fighting of the Civil War while his only child was still a baby. He joined the First Louisiana Cavalry of the *Union* Army. He was wounded three times, and first came to New Orleans as a soldier in the Union Army in 1862.

His service on the Union side made the senior Hennessy a hated man when he stayed in New Orleans after the war. The city's favorite hero in those days was its most admired resident, former Confederate General Pierre Gustave Toutant de Beauregard. Beauregard had been in command of the guns that fired the first shots on Fort Sumter, and thereby began a war that was to kill more than twice as many Americans as were killed in World War II—at a time when the American population was only 28 to 30 million.

The South's rage after its defeat was aggravated in New Orleans by the city's special experience. Early in the war, in April 1862, a Union fleet commanded by Admiral David G. Farragut astonished everyone by fighting its way past the blazing guns of the Confederate forts, Jackson and St. Philip, across from each other on the Mississippi River, cut a massive steel chain which spanned the river, and captured New Orleans before its citizens could organize their defenses. The city spent the rest of the war under an iron-fisted Union occupation. Upon taking over New Orleans, the Union Army lost no time in showing its rebellious residents who was boss. A famous statue of Andrew Jackson on horseback had stood in the Place d'Armes, the historical heart of New Orleans, since it was unveiled in 1856 and the Place was renamed Jackson Square. The army ordered that a certain quotation from Jackson be deeply chiseled into the pedestal of the statue, where the bold letters can still be seen today. It reads: *"The Union Must and Shall Be Preserved."*

It is difficult today to appreciate the hatred the people of the city bore toward the Union occupiers, a hatred which conditioned events there for decades afterward. It was so bad that the city's women took to spitting at the soldiers, a popular practice which provoked the army's commanding general to issue an extraordinary order on May 15, 1862:

> . . . it is ordered that hereafter when any female shall, by word, gesture, or movement, insult or show contempt for any officer or soldier of the United States, she shall be regarded and held liable to be treated as a woman of the town plying her avocation.

After the war, the senior Hennessy became a policeman on the despised Metropolitan Police force, an instrument of federal Reconstruction carpetbaggers, under the command of General Algernon S. Badger, later a member of the Committee of Fifty. As a general in the Union cavalry, Badger, a Northerner, had been the senior Hennessy's commanding officer. He was given command of the Metropolitan Police after the war, and appointed the senior Hennessy to its ranks.

Although they were the Police Department of the city of New Orleans, the Metropolitans were under the direct command of the Governor of the state of Louisiana, an arrangement of the Reconstruction program designed to keep control of the South firmly in the hands of Northerners and their southern collaborators. One of the most passionate enemies of the Metropolitans was Arthur Guerin, an unreconstructed Confederate enthusiast. Guerin regarded Hennessy, former Union soldier and now Metropolitan policeman, as an oppressor twice over. The hatred came to a boil in 1867. According to one version, a wild gunfight broke out between the two men in a saloon. While the bar's other patrons dived for cover, the two men exchanged several shots. In another account of what happened, Hennessy was in the bar drinking with a friend when Guerin suddenly shot him, without warning. In either case, Hennessy, in the phrase of many popular ballads of the time, ended up "dead on the barroom floor." Guerin was not punished for the killing, but was himself killed several years later in another private shoot-out on the stairs of the old Civil District Court building.

Young David Hennessy was left fatherless. In 1870, his father's commander, General Badger, gave the eleven-year-old boy a job in his office as a messenger. As Badger was later fond of saying, the boy proved to be so clever, diligent, and courageous that he frequently promoted him during the next years. When Badger was forced from command of the department in 1875 by anti-Reconstructionist forces, seventeen-year-old Hennessy was one of the only two men the General insisted must stay on the force. The entire force was reorganized under its new chief, Thomas N. Boylan, appointed by a newly elected anti-Reconstructionist governor of Louisiana, Francis T. Nicholls. Boylan and Hennessy soon were close friends.

Hennessy's career rose, as did his local fame, through sensational exploits. For example, while still a teen-ager he caught two grown men in the act of theft, single-handedly beat them in a street fight, and dragged them to a police station.

The two-fisted young man was made a detective before his twenty-first birthday. Many years ago, one of his admirers, the aforementioned Louisiana historian, John S. Kendall, described him at about this age. "Dave," said Kendall, "was a typical policeman of the old regime—a man of iron nerves, implacable, unscrupulous, who would have been what we nowadays call a 'gangster' if he had not happened to line up on the side of law and order. He was a tall, stalwart man, handsome after the human bull-dog style, with a heavy black mustache and abundant, well-oiled black hair combed down in a curve low on his forehead."

The young detective was soon to be famous throughout the United States and Europe for something he did in 1881, when he was but twenty-three years old.

Hennessy's international fame was born July 5, 1881. On that

28

afternoon, four detectives followed a short, powerfully built, broad-shouldered Italian as he walked along the New Orleans riverfront near Canal Street. The man strolled casually, stopping to exchange a few words now and then with fellow Italians, who formed the predominant population in this part of the city. When the man reached an empty spot about fifty yards from Jackson Square, the four plainclothesmen drew pistols and jumped him. The surprised man was unarmed, and surrendered without a struggle. He was Giuseppe Esposito, an infamous criminal wanted by the police in Italy for several murders and kidnappings. Of the four cops who captured him, two were private detectives hired in New York City by the Italian Government. The other two were New Orleans' own David Hennessy and his cousin, Detective Michael Hennessy, who, although he was older, was David's henchman.

The fugitive Esposito had come to the Hennessys' attention five months before. In March, a newspaperman by chance witnessed a fight between an Italian man and a pretty Italian woman outside a small Italian restaurant on Customhouse Street. Not knowing a word of Italian, the reporter watched as the woman shouted in the foreign tongue and gesticulated in angry motions, answered now and then by the man with short Italian phrases and sharp gestures. Suddenly the woman picked up a bottle from the street and pitched it at the man. It shattered on a post near his head. With a quick angry gesture, the man grabbed the woman and drew her to him. Then he kissed her, or as the reporter told it, "scraped her flushed cheeks with his two weeks' growth of scrubby black beard." The Italian turned to the reporter with a smile and said in broken English, "Ah, these women! What can you do with these women?"

It was a colorful happening, but hardly worthy of attention in hurly-burly New Orleans. Except that in the rapid words the woman had shouted, the reporter thought he had picked out the single word *bandito*. The newsman told the story to two members of the Police Department he knew would not let it rest, the ambitious Dave and Mike Hennessy.

29

The Hennessys soon learned that the Italian called himself Joe Randazzo and lived with a wife and three children in a rented slum apartment on Chartres Street, between St. Philip and Dumaine. They also learned that he liked to spend time with two friends in Joseph Raphael's Italian restaurant on Burgundy and Customhouse streets. Raphael was Italian, and the Hennessys got him to eavesdrop on the subject's conversation with his buddies. Raphael reported back that the three men spoke an Italian dialect which he did not understand. This was not unusual. The dialects throughout Italy varied greatly (and still do) from region to region, sometimes from town to town. In fact, Esposito was from an area of Sicily where an old Albanian or "Arbreshe," population spoke a dialect which was imcomprehensible even to their neighbors. Unaware of Italy's dialects, the Hennessys became convinced that the three men were using a "thieves' jargon," an imagined special language created by Italian criminals so that they could talk without fear of being understood by others.

On the basis of this misunderstanding, the Hennessys hired an artist to sit in Raphael's restaurant and secretly make a sketch of their suspect. They turned the portrait over to the Italian Consulate for transmission to the police in Italy. Several weeks passed while the Hennessys shadowed their man and waited for word from Italy. When it came, it delighted the cousins. Their suspect was none other than Giuseppe Esposito, the most infamous fugitive in all of Europe.

The Italian Government urged the Hennessys not to take action yet, a request with which the detectives could easily comply. They had not told anyone in the New Orleans police about their investigation of the suspicious Italian, except their friend the Chief of Police.

The Italian Government had been looking for Esposito for two years, and wanted him too much for anything to go wrong. Because Esposito's last crime in Italy had raised a great deal of horror in foreign countries, England especially, it was a matter of Italy's honor that he be brought to justice by Italian authorities.

Two years before the Hennessys found Esposito in New Orleans, an Englishman named John Forrester Rose was kidnapped by a group of bandits while traveling in Italy and taken to a mountain hideout. The leader of the mountain bandits was called Leone (Lion). His second in command was Giuseppe Esposito.

Rose, according to some accounts, was the son of a wealthy banking family, and an absentee landholder in Sicily who had gone there to inspect his properties. Other stories describe him, not necessarily in contradiction, as a Protestant minister.

Leone sent a ransom note to Rose's wife, demanding 5,000 British pounds. To make it more impressive, he cut off one of her husband's ears and enclosed it in the envelope. (The same technique was used by kidnappers in Italy's Calabrian mountains in 1973 when they cut off one of the ears of the grandson of oil billionaire John Paul Getty and sent it to his grandfather.) The British were outraged, and demanded that the Italian Government move against the bandits, which it did. This led to another letter to Mrs. Rose, containing her husband's other ear and part of his nose. The terrified woman paid the ransom, and her mutilated husband was released.

It happened that while they had been holding the Englishman, Leone's band raided the villa of an Italian prince, intending to take him for ransom too. The prince escaped the attackers, who took instead the prince's house guest, an American. When he arrived at the bandit hideout, the American protested that he was just a poor artist. The skeptical bandits ordered him to prove his story by drawing a portrait of one of the band—Esposito. Esposito was disappointed that they had taken a man without wealth, but he liked the picture. The kidnappers decided to hold the artist, chiefly because they needed someone to write letters in English to Mrs. Rose.

The artist's first ransom note, the one that accompanied the minister's first ear, was written on the back of the sketch of Esposito. According to the artist, Esposito sent it out of vanity, wanting the world to know what a good-looking fellow he was. In fact, according to one unlikely version, Esposito was so pleased with the publicity the portrait gave him that when the artist was

31

released unharmed (after his friend the prince paid a ransom), the bandit handed the American back the full ransom. It was this work of the American artist done in a Sicilian cave that was to lead to Esposito's final capture in New Orleans two years later, after it had been matched with the second portrait sent by the Hennessys.

Esposito's hard times started as soon as Rose was released. In response to a clamor from the British, the Italian Army set off on a campaign to wipe out Leone's band. They had done so several times over the years, but now they were in dead earnest. Their opportunity came when someone sold out the bandits, telling the authorities where they were. A full *brigata* of cavalry, artillery, and infantry regiments surrounded the band, whose number, said to be at one time from 60 to 160, had been reduced to just 16 men. The troops opened fire and didn't stop until all the bandits were cut down. Nine of them, including Leone, were dead. The other seven, including Esposito, were seriously wounded. The soldiers put the wounded in guarded wagons for the trip out of the mountains. On the way, the soldiers explained in a hard-to-believe report, Esposito, despite serious wounds, somehow jumped out of an enclosed wagon and fled on foot, under a shower of bullets. After the army chased him in vain around the mountains, the Italian Government offered a reward of 25,000 lire ($5,000) for information leading to his capture.

Somehow Esposito escaped to New York, and then made his way to New Orleans. He changed his name to Randazzo, and bought a lugger, or small fishing boat, which he named *Leone* after his dead friend. However, he spent his days selling fruits and vegetables from a pushcart on Customhouse Street, between Burgundy and Rampart. He soon married a young Italian widow with two children. The couple then had a third child of their own.

Things were going well for the fugitive, who, despite claims made years later that he was a powerful Mafia boss in New Orleans, lived on a humble level. In any case, he lived without any signs of wealth. It was said that he lavished love on the three children and his wife. He might someday have died peacefully as an old man in New Orleans' "Little Palermo" had it not been for the fact that he already had a wife back in Sicily. According to the Italian authorities, the first wife, feeling deserted, told them that Esposito was in New Orleans. In the spring of 1881, the Italian Consulate in New York wrote to the New Orleans police asking them to watch for Esposito. Thus, when the newsman told the Hennessys about the street fight between the Italian couple, the two detectives had already been alerted that Esposito might be in New Orleans by their friend and Chief, Colonel Boylan.

Desire for glory made the Hennessys eager to cooperate with the Italian Government when it became clear that the detectives were on to Esposito. The cousins agreed to a plan devised by the Italians, and waited for the arrival of the two New York private detectives hired by the foreign government.

The plan was as simple as it was bold, and it was quickly carried out. The Hennessys and the two New York cops quietly took Esposito to a police station just across Jackson Square. He was locked up without being booked, to maintain secrecy. After nightfall, the four cops drove the manacled Italian around the city on the floor of a carriage to lose anyone who might be following them. Under cover of darkness, the detectives rowed the bandit in a small skiff from the foot of Canal Street to a ship bound for New York, appropriately named *City of New Orleans*. There was a perfunctory extradition hearing in New York, at which Esposito's New Orleans wife and friends tried to convince the authorities that the arrested man was the individual, then dead, to whom she had formerly been married. These perjurers included Giuseppe Provenzano and Rocco Geraci of New Orleans, the latter of whom was among a group ambushed by the Provenzanos and was to become one of those accused in Hennessy's murder, both some nine years later.

Newspapers also reported the rumor that Esposito's friends in New Orleans raised $5,000 for his defense. Nine years later, just after David Hennessy's murder, his secretary, George W. Vandervoort, told reporters that during the hearing Hennessy had been offered bribes of more than $50,000 by Italians. Although Vandervoort didn't produce any evidence whatsoever to confirm the story, it was widely accepted as true. Few seemed to wonder that a man who could command $50,000, a fabulous sum by 1881 standards, would live with his family in a slum and continue to sell fruit every day from a pushcart stand. The New Orleans *Daily Picayune* typified American newspaper attitudes when it reported that "the moral fiber of the policeman was evidenced by his refusal of the Mafia bribes."

Esposito was placed on board a waiting Italian warship, which immediately sailed for Italy. In December 1881, he was tried in Palermo, Sicily, on eighteen counts of murder and one hundred counts of kidnapping and extortion. He was found guilty of six murders, and sentenced to death. But because the Italian Parliament in the previous decade had voted to abolish capital punishment, Italy's King commuted the sentence to life imprisonment. Esposito was placed in a fortress-like prison, where he eventually died of natural causes. Seven years after Esposito's expulsion to Italy, his New Orleans wife, who was now living in Louisville, applied for her children to be entered in a municipal orphanage, explaining that she could no longer support them on her earnings as a laundry woman. This ending, too, casts doubt on the stories that Esposito was a wealthy leader of the New Orleans Mafia instead of a petty, if vicious, criminal.

News of Esposito's capture had first broken when he arrived in New York. An Italian steward on board the ship to New York had been called into the stateroom where Esposito was chained to act as interpreter. The steward broke the story when the ship docked, telling how Esposito had been "kidnapped" while his wife and children stood crying at dockside. Without sentimentality, the Hennessys replied that the bandit's family didn't even know of the capture until the prisoner was on the seas on his way to New York.

The Italian-Americans of New Orleans and New York, many of whom believed the wife's claim that her husband was not Esposito, were angered by the steward's story and raised money, probably less than the reported $5,000, to fight Esposito's extradition to Italy.

Except for the Italian immigrant communities in cities around the United States, no one raised any objection to the way Esposito had been disposed of. There was no objection that the laws of the state of Louisiana had been broken. Nor was there any protest that, even by the casual standards of 1881, Esposito's most fundamental legal rights under the U. S. Constitution had been violated. Normally a foreign government's kidnapping of a resident of the United States on American soil would be considered extremely offensive. Yet the federal government in Washington didn't enter a demurer. Even after the prisoner had been conclusively proved to be Esposito, obvious conclusions were drawn about due process and equality under America law by Italian-Americans and other immigrant groups. And by the year 1900, immigrants and their children made up a full one third of the American population.

As a result of the Esposito affair, David Hennessy was celebrated as a model of American manhood throughout the United States, Great Britain, and continental Europe. The largely sensationalistic press of the time embroidered the facts of the case. Wild stories were printed of secret "stiletto" and "vendetta" Italian "societies" in the United States, and largely ignorant accounts of the Mafia and Camorra in Italy became favorite reading at the American breakfast table. Newspaper readers all over the world learned that the foremost American "expert" on these nefarious organizations was David Hennessy. Hennessy said nothing to qualify the fantastic stories that were catapulting him to international celebrity.

The young Hennessy's future now seemed assured. His ambitions could soar—some newspapers were already saying that the twenty-three-year-old policeman would make a fine senator, and that this southern son of a Union hero might someday even make a fine American President! Hennessy's fame was such that in New Orleans it even eclipsed that of the city's perennial favorite, the now fading, white-haired, sixty-three-year-old General Beauregard.

Yet just nine months after Esposito's capture, David Hennessy was to find himself forced to resign from the Police Department in bitter disgrace, his career seemingly at a dead end. The cause? Once again, death-dealing violence. Buoyed by the success of the Esposito affair, Hennessy, with the support of his cousin Mike, began a campaign to get the highly political Police Board to appoint him Chief of Detectives. This would have put him in position to succeed Thomas Boylan, who was soon to retire, as Police Chief. Boylan himself, who was later a member of the Committee of Fifty, publicly supported Hennessy in this ambition.

However, not long after the Esposito case, Boylan and the Hennessys became infuriated when one of David Hennessy's rivals, Thomas Devereaux, was appointed by the board as head of the detective squad. The politically well-connected Devereaux was not even, nor had he ever been, on the police force.

A bitter contest began between David Hennessy and Devereaux over who was to take command from Boylan as Chief. The Police Board was an arena for the fight. Its meetings became increasingly heated as the two factions and their board supporters struggled for power. But it was not the only arena; nor were Hennessy and Devereaux the only contenders for the position. Another detective, Robert Harris of the New Orleans police, also sought it. Like his rivals, he too had support on the board as well as in the department.

Devereaux ended the third detective's competition in a typical New Orleans manner. One day, in broad daylight, he blew Harris' brains all over a street with his heavy, hair-triggered Tranier pistol which fired an unusually large bullet. Devereaux claimed it was self-defense. His enemies called it murder. Devereaux was not tried, and remained Chief of Detectives.

Devereaux now locked horns with the Hennessys, and the struggle between them became more vicious. On a number of occasions, Mike Hennessy, a hot-tempered man unlike his cool-headed cousin, publicly exchanged abusive words with the chief detective.

The feud came to a boil when Devereaux accused Mike Hennessy before the Police Board of being insubordinate, and demanded that he be fired. When the board dismissed the charges, Devereaux became enraged and gave the board a tongue-lashing. For this, the board ordered *him* to stand trial for insolence and insubordination. Rubbing salt in the wound, the board scheduled Mike Hennessy as a witness against him.

The matter was resolved on October 13, 1881, just four months after Hennessy became an international celebrity. On that day, Devereaux was in the office of John W. Fairfax, the editor of the New Orleans *City Item* and a major stockbroker. As Fairfax later testified, he, Devereaux, and a businessman with political connections named Maurice J. Hart (later a member of the Committee of Fifty) were standing in his ground-floor office discussing investments. According to Fairfax's sworn testimony, Mike Hennessy suddenly appeared at the window with a drawn pistol and fired a shot through the glass into the office. Devereaux pulled his quick-firing horse pistol and shot back just as Dave Hennessy was seen by Fairfax next to his cousin, firing at the Chief of Detectives. At this point, Fairfax jumped behind a large office safe for protection. Several shots more were fired from inside and outside the window. Suddenly David Hennessy burst into the side door of the office and fired a single pistol shot at close range into Devereaux's head. Fairfax claimed the Chief of Detectives was making for another door when gunned down.

After looking down at his dead rival, David Hennessy unhurriedly holstered his pistol under his jacket and went outside. His cousin lay on the sidewalk, moaning. A bullet had entered his mouth, shattered three of his teeth, exited through one of his cheeks, and finally lodged in his neck. David picked him up and brought him to Charity Hospital, where he eventually recovered.

The next five months saw behind-the-scenes political attempts by Hennessy supporters to get Devereaux's killing declared justified self-defense. But the damning statements of Fairfax and others on the front pages of many newspapers in the United States created too much pressure. Finally, six months later, in April 1882, David and Michael Hennessy went on trial for murder.

At the trial the police testified that they found Mike Hennessy's

Colt revolver with two empty chambers, and Devereaux's Tranier, which had fired four shots. In response to a question, they disclosed that no one had examined Dave Hennessy's pistol after the shooting to see if he had fired only one shot, as he claimed.

Fairfax repeated his testimony on the stand, insisting under cross-examination that Devereaux had not made a move for his pistol until after the first shot, which came through the window from Mike Hennessy outside.

David Hennessy testified that he and his cousin happened coincidentally to be walking past Fairfax's office, not knowing Devereaux was there. Suddenly a shot crashed through the office window from the inside. David headed for the door at the side of the office. On his way, he heard several more shots. With his pistol cocked and raised he burst into the room to see Devereaux standing at the window, aiming his pistol at his cousin, who lay on the sidewalk just outside. David immediately fired one shot—the only one he claimed to have fired that day—and Devereaux fell. His entrance and shot had been so fast, he said, that the Chief of Detectives didn't have a chance to turn from the window, explaining why the shot entered his left ear. Mike Hennessy corroborated Dave's story.

Both the state and the defense produced witnesses to the shooting, who on each side only partially corroborated the contradictory accounts of Fairfax and the Hennessys. Maurice J. Hart, the man who had been standing with Devereaux and Fairfax when the shooting started, testified that Devereaux drew his weapon before the Hennessys drew theirs. Upon prosecution cross-examination, it was established that this was different testimony from that which he had given before to a grand jury. He had *not* told the grand jury that Devereaux drew first. He also admitted that he had talked to the Hennessys earlier on the day of the shooting. His insistence that the first shots were fired "simultaneously" by Devereaux and Michael Hennessy and that he did not see David Hennessy shoot Devereaux, because he, Hart, was hiding behind office furniture, undercut Fairfax's testimony and the prosecution's case.

Each side produced witnesses to establish motives. A friend of both Devereaux and the Hennessys testified that three or four days before the shooting Devereaux made threats against the lives of the Hennessys. He told this to the cousins the next day. Another witness swore that four or five days before he was killed, Devereaux said to him about the Hennessys, "They may get the best of me before the Police Board, but if they do, I'll get a double barreled gun and blow their heads off." The Hennessys had been informed of the threat. A policeman testified that he also heard Devereaux threaten to kill the Hennessys and that he too told them about it.

The prosecution called witnesses who swore they saw the Hennessys near Devereaux's house on the morning of the shooting. The defense countered that they went there looking for the man, who was their boss, on official business, to deliver some documents to him. Mike Hennessy's sister supported the claim by declaring that she was present when her brother and cousin came to Mike's house on the morning of the shooting to get the papers.

The defense lawyers placed great emphasis upon Devereaux's reputation for bad temper and violence, and contrasted it with the cool heroism and fine character of David Hennessy, the career policeman who had so recently "risked the revenge of the Mafia" in bringing the fugitive Esposito to justice.

On April 26, the jury was locked up and deliberated through the night. After nineteen hours, the twelve men returned to the court.

The jury foreman boomed out the verdict. "Not guilty!"

There was absolute stillness in the court. Then David Hennessy smiled. No one moved.

Despite the acquittal, the affair had caused such a national scandal that even New Orleans had to bend to it. Public opinion forced Chief Boylan, against his will, to ask for the resignation of both Hennessys from the police force.

Michael Hennessy left New Orleans for good, making his way to Texas. Three years later, he was shot to death in a personal brawl in Houston.

For the first time since he was eleven years old, twenty-four-year-old David Hennessy was no longer working for the New Orleans police force. He was just a private citizen. But not for long. Shortly after the trial, he joined the private Farrell Protection Police as a bank detective. In effect, Hennessy was back with the municipal police, for in 1880 the Mayor and City Council had commissioned Farrell policemen "as patrolmen with police powers," that is, in reality as equals to the city police. A few months later Thomas Boylan retired as city Police Chief and formed the powerful Boylan Protective Police. Boylan's co-founder and second-in-command was David C. Hennessy. The City Council then turned the Farrell police's public contract over to the Boylan police. Hennessy was now, in fact, the second most powerful policeman in New Orleans, right behind the city department's Chief—exactly the position that he and Boylan tried to get for him after he killed Devereaux.

David Hennessy's favored position in the city's politics is seen in the fact that he, and not the municipal Police Chief or any of the other, private, forces, was given the prestigious job of heading security at the famous New Orleans World's Fair in 1884–85. The fair, which celebrated the one hundredth anniversary of the first American shipment of cotton to England, was housed in a gigantic exhibition hall covering thirty-three acres. It was touted as the largest building in the world at the time.

The upward path for Hennessy was to continue to be heavily involved with the complicated, poisoned politics of the city and Police Department of New Orleans. This path—including Hennessy's killing of Chief Devereaux, and his self-seeking, illegal behavior in the Esposito case—vanished in the accounts of him given after his death.

7

The myth of heroism and martyrdom thrown around Hennessy's memory had an immediate effect upon one of the mourners passing his casket on the morning of his funeral, a twenty-nine-year-old newspaper peddler named Thomas Duffy. On occasion, the late Chief had bought a paper from him. Although this was the only association Duffy claimed with the dead man, he became enraged by the popular accounts of his murder.

After participating in the emotionally charged procession past the coffin, the overage newsboy walked around the city, passing an exhibit of crayon drawings of Hennessy at the entrance of the Grand Opera House, which had been set up literally over night. His next stop was Parish Prison.

The events that followed underlined the Committee of Fifty's threatening letter against Italian-Americans, which was printed five days later. They bear a startling resemblance to those which occurred seventy-three years later at the Dallas police headquarters following the murder of John F. Kennedy.

It was visitors' day at the prison, and Duffy presented himself to the guards at the "bull pen" area of the institution, an enclosure between the inner and outer gates, and asked to see a certain prisoner. Duffy had visited the man before, and was taken inside the prison without question. After spending a few minutes with the man, Duffy came out into the bull pen again. He told the four guards present that he had read that a man named "Scafiro" had been arrested for shooting Hennessy, and that he could identify him as one of the killers. One of the guards went in to get Antonio Scaffidi. Duffy paced around in a circle while he waited, his right hand inside his jacket.

"What've you got for the dago," joked one of the guards, "a bomb?"

"No," answered Duffy seriously.

Just then Scaffidi appeared at the bars of the inner gate. Upon Duffy's request, the Italian opened his jacket. The newspaper seller charged toward him with a modern .32-caliber revolver in his hand. The four guards pounced on him, but not before he fired a shot. Duffy and the guards struggled, rolling over one another on the ground. The gunman was finally pinned face down to the ground and disarmed. He shouted, "If there were seventy-five more men like me in New Orleans, we'd run all the dagoes out of the city!" The warden, Captain Davis, was summoned.

The warden arrived in a moment to find Scaffidi twisting violently on the ground, making horrible choking sounds. Duffy's bullet had hit him in the neck, entering the right side of his throat about an inch and a half to the side of the windpipe, passing just next to the carotid artery, and apparently finally lodging in the muscles at the back of the neck. Davis phoned for an ambulance. He was furious with his men, and gave them a tongue-lashing on the spot, ordering that in the future all people visiting Italian prisoners be first searched.

At Charity Hospital, doctors decided that it would be too dangerous to try to remove the bullet from Scaffidi's throat. They dressed the wound, bandaged his neck, and placed him on a bed in a ward. They did not give him anything for his pain.

At 1:30 P.M., reporters found the wounded Italian "twitching violently with pain," unattended except for two guards from the prison. The guards had accompanied him from the prison with orders from Warden Davis to protect him. (Davis stayed behind because a mob had gathered outside the prison on a rumor that "one of the dagoes made a break.") Instead, they let anyone and everyone get next to his bed and told reporters they were there "to prevent his escaping." Scaffidi's black mustache and curly hair were shining with sweat, and his dark eyes were wild with pain and fear. He pleaded, "I won't make a break!" The bulky bandages around his neck made the thrashing man appear as if he were being strangled to death by some large snake. "I'm dying," he told the reporters in English. "Please, send for my parents and my sisters. I've lived here for ten years and never was in trouble. I'm twenty-four years old, and here they kill me like a dog."

A reporter asked, "Are you suffering very much?"

"Yes, in the head and chest. Please get a priest."

Instead of a priest, two judges arrived with a male stenographer to question the wounded man. "How do you do, Scaffidi," one said.

"You know me, Judge," Scaffidi pleaded. "Haven't I always been a good man?"

"Well, Scaffidi, I do know you," answered the judge, acknowledging an acquaintance never explained, "but my present mission is not to recall acquaintances. I have come to ask you if you think you are going to die, and in that case, if you wish to make a declaration."

"Oh yes, yes, I believe I am going to die, but I die innocent! Before God, I declare I am innocent. I know nothing of the killing. I do not know who did it. I had no bad feelings against the Chief. If I knew who killed him, I would tell you."

He extended his hand toward the judge, who, refusing to take it, turned without another word and left the hospital with his two companions. Finally Warden Davis arrived and cleared everyone away from Scaffidi, who was allowed a visit by his mother and sister.

The reporters told the police what Scaffidi said. The police countered that while Scaffidi had no criminal record, they believed him to be involved in a case of extortion and a second case of extortion and murder. But they had no evidence to offer.

Although the bullet was never removed from his throat, Scaffidi recovered from his wound. Thomas Duffy was eventually tried for assault with a deadly weapon with intent to commit murder, a charge which could have meant *life in prison* under Louisiana law. He was convicted, and sentenced to six months in Parish Prison.

8

After threatening all the city's Italian-Americans in its public letter, the Committee of Fifty's next move was to have another fourteen of them indicted for Hennessy's murder, in addition to the five charged the day after the assassination. (The names of the nineteen indicted men are in Appendix E.) The Committee announced that the murder resulted from a large conspiracy by Italians. New Orleans was startled by the Committee's charge that the ringleader was a prestigious, wealthy man named Joseph P. Macheca.

Macheca was born in Louisiana of Sicilian parents and adopted in infancy by a Maltese man, whose name he took. Macheca's stepfather pioneered the business of importing fresh fruit from Latin America and citrus fruit from Italy. The stepson was sole owner of the shipping line, inherited from his stepfather, and his business dominated the lucrative docks of New Orleans. The forty-seven-year-old Macheca had been active in New Orleans politics all his life, and for the past eight years was Consul of Bolivia, an honorary title. In 1874, as a captain in Company B of the First Louisiana Infantry Regiment of the state militia, he took part in the "battle of Liberty Place," the fighting in the streets against the Metropolitan Police which cost 27 killed and 100 wounded and which threw out the hated Reconstructionist government from the city. The regiment was a citizens' reserve army, of contested legality, made up substantially of former Confederate soldiers. In the fighting, the regiment allied itself with the Crescent City White League, whose leaders led the 1874 take-over and whose members were to have prominent places on the Committee of Fifty sixteen years later. The League was organized after the

Civil War under the command of a former Confederate general. Its purposes were to force an end to Reconstruction and to suppress both blacks and the white working-class labor movement. (Although either Macheca, or his stepfather, who died in 1878, led a political group of 150 Sicilians in an earlier, violent anti-black demonstration, neither was not a member of the White League.)

In the 1874 battle, Macheca distinguished himself by saving the life of the wounded "enemy" commander, Metropolitan Police Chief Algernon S. Badger—Hennessy's mentor. A mob recruited by the White League had captured him and were about to kill the wounded man when Macheca, commanding a group of the Louisiana Regiment, intervened. For this Macheca won a medal—and the hatred of at least some in the League.

To explain the motive behind the conspiracy which they charged Macheca headed, the Committee of Fifty raised an incident that had occurred a few months before. It had linked David Hennessy once again with the city's Italians in a sensational—and very questionable—way.

A bitter rivalry was being fought out between two groups of Italian stevedores for work on the New Orleans docks. One group was led by the Provenzano family (Joseph, George, Vincent, and Peter), and the other by the Mantranga brothers, Charles and Anthony. Although the Committee of Fifty and the Mayor were later to charge that this was a "Mafia" struggle, it was in reality a contest between two labor cliques, very much like the labor violence of our day. Both Italian groups were prone to the typical violence of the city at the time, and in fact merely perpetuated the rough and crude New Orleans longshore ways of operating they took over from their Irish-American predecessors. In addition, both the Provenzanos and the Mantrangas were reputed to be involved in the city's common corruption and related crime in much the same ways as were many of New Orleans' leading non-Italian powers. To label the same behavior "Mafia" when done by Italians and something else when done by others is a confusing and frightening practice indulged in in gilded age New Orleans, and today as well.

There is little doubt that the Provenzanos and Mantrangas were rough and unsavory people, but no more so than the typical leaders in New Orleans' labor, politics, or the police force at the time—and, we might add, considerably less powerful than these others. Labor, business, and political corruption was notoriously common to American cities in the 1890s. And it was by no means limited to immigrant political "machines" as some history books suggest. The native-born Anglo-Saxon government and other institutions of Philadelphia comprised a system as corrupt as immigrant-ridden New Orleans, New York, and Chicago. In 1890, the Provenzanos and the Mantrangas were primarily *padroni*— "bosses" who exploited Italian laborers.

As the city's leading Italian in politics and richest Italian, Macheca had been trying to mediate the dispute between the Provenzanos and Mantrangas when it exploded on May 6, 1890. At 12:30 A.M. on that date, a group of Mantranga longshoremen were ambushed as they rode in a wagon from the docks. (The names of the men are in Appendix F.) Three of them were wounded by gunfire, the most serious being Anthony Mantranga, whose wound required the amputation of a leg. The group swore they had seen their assailants and identified them as members of the Provenzano faction.

Police Chief Hennessy was at the scene a few minutes after the shooting and, in response to the public accusations of the victims, ordered the arrest of twelve men in the rival group, including the four Provenzanos. (The names of the twelve are in Appendix G.)

At the trial of six of these men, two months later, Macheca played a key role. He gave the prosecution its motive by testifying that the Provenzanos were angry because he had recently transferred his business from them to the Mantranga stevedores. This testimony was cited after Hennessy's murder by the Committee of Fifty as proof that Macheca was allied with the Mantrangas.

The Provenzano trial was a curious one. The judge threw a private detective out of the courtroom upon a complaint from a defense lawyer that the man had been "motioning" to one of the jurors. The juror denied knowing the private cop or having anything to do with him, but because the defense raised the question, the impression was given that someone was trying to influence the juror *against* the accused.

But the thing about the trial that drew most attention was the fact that so many policemen testified for the defense, and seemed to be "reaching" to give the accused an alibi. According to unconfirmed accounts, Hennessy and the Provenzanos were part owners of a whorehouse called, appropriately, the Red Lantern Club, located near Hennessy's home in an area so violent it was popularly known as "the Swamp." Rumors that Hennessy was allied with the Provenzanos and had ordered his men to "get them off" were so thick that after the six Italians were found guilty on July 18 (and sentenced to *life imprisonment*), a special grand jury was hastily assembled to investigate police involvement. After less than a week of listening to unchallenged testimony from several high-ranking policemen—but not Hennessy, who had not been called—the jury announced on July 31 that it had found "no dereliction of duty" on the part of the police.

Lawyers for the Provenzanos petitioned for a new trial, and the city was surprised in August 1890 when the same judge who had tried them granted what had been sought. The newspapers noted widespread suspicions that someone powerful was pushing in favor of the Provenzanos, for no new evidence had been introduced in the petition for a new trial to justify the judge's decision. That someone, rumors had it, was Chief Hennessy. For several weeks after, newspapers were filled with rumors that Hennessy would testify at the new trial and offer some mysterious evidence proving the Provenzanos' innocence. Although the Chief said nothing to confirm these rumors, he did nothing to dispel them. Hennessy was killed exactly one week before the date set for the new trial, and Mayor Shakspeare and the Committee of Fifty said he had been murdered to prevent his testifying. When the second trial was actually held, three months later, the story was so widely believed that a jury found the Provenzano group innocent on January 23, 1891, upon the same evidence that had convicted them at their first trial. No one ever brought forth Hennessy's "evidence."

The charge that he was "silenced" to prevent his disclosing "Mafia secrets he had uncovered" was nonetheless accepted as fact.

Until the Provenzano-Mantranga shooting, Hennessy and Macheca had been friends. They had been seen together at the "men's club" with the colorful name, the Red Lantern Club. Witnesses reported they had a falling out because Macheca objected to Hennessy's becoming involved as a partisan favoring the Provenzanos in their struggle with the Mantrangas. Macheca's alleged warning to Hennessy that the rivalry was "strictly an Italian affair" and that Hennessy should stay out of it, together with hostile remarks Macheca was supposed to have made about Hennessy on the night of his death, was the only "evidence" the Committee of Fifty introduced to substantiate its charges against him.

Whether Hennessy was killed in a struggle arising out of New Orleans politics or the politics of the police force—possibilities never considered—or whether the gunmen and their employers were actually Italian, the murder was seized upon by the New Orleans political and commercial powers as an opportunity to destroy the rising economic power and social threat of the Italian community. The plan was simple. By destroying Joseph Macheca, New Orleans' most prestigious and wealthy Italian, and by persecuting the entire Italian community, the "dagoes" would be put in their place. And Macheca's very profitable waterfront influence could be taken over by "responsible" citizens, some of whom, as we shall see, were principal persecutors of the Italians.

Thus Macheca was charged as the head of the conspiracy. Charles Mantranga was charged as "his lieutenant," and twelve employees or former employees of the Mantranga brothers, including three men who had been victims in the attack on May 6, 1890, for which five Provenzano men had been convicted and then acquitted, were charged as accomplices, along with the five Italians already charged with being the actual gunmen.

9

Joseph Macheca was the most prominent and powerful of thirty thousand Italian-Americans in the New Orleans area in 1890. By that year they made up more than one tenth of the population, and by 1930 they were the largest of sixteen white ethnic groups in the city surveyed by the U. S. Bureau of the Census (counting foreign-born residents and their children). Some 70 percent of them had made the long voyage from Sicily in "cattle car" immigrant ships in the years since 1880. Their sudden flux from Sicily in the 1880s created dramatic changes in the Crescent City. Thousands of Italians came to the city—5,644 during the years 1891 and 1892 alone, all but 62 of them Sicilians. In a dozen years, most of the city's heart, the French Quarter, was transformed as the Sicilians settled there among blacks and residues of the poor among older Irish- and German-American populations.

Two of the three traditional "sights" of the city were completely taken over by Italians. The famous French Market had become, in fact, an Italian market, resembling those found in the Porta di Castro area of Palermo, Sicily. The market, built in 1813, was a long one-story building with a peaked slate roof supported by wide Doric columns made of brick and plastered over to look like coarse marble. One visitor of the period said the structure looked like a gigantic "rookery," a word for the crowded breeding grounds of certain birds which had recently been pressed into use to describe the tenement slums of American cities.

The market was divided into three sections. The first area had sides of meat hanging from every inch of the rafters holding up the distinctive roof. In this period before refrigeration in hot, humid New Orleans, the smell was said to turn the stomachs of veteran slaughterhouse workers.

The riot of smells in the second area came from the things jammed into its stalls, from strong fish and wild-game meat to musty vegetables, pungent fruits, and sweet flowers. The city's many Italian pushcart peddlers, or, as they called themselves, "walking peddlers," picked up their produce here at dawn. Much of the city depended on the Italian-controlled market for its food supply.

The third section of the market featured dry goods, and was a clothing center, especially for the poor. (The only part of the old market which remained unchanged was the marble coffee stands run by black women wearing brightly colored Creole scarves tied around their hair to form chignons, or *'tignons,* at the nape of the neck.) The market not only fed the city; it was also highly dependent on the Macheca Shipping Line for its produce. It is located on Decatur Street, whose entire length running along the riverfront was a jumble of Italian signs and Italian sounds.

To the new immigrants, the ramshackle wooden buildings of Decatur Street made up a transplanted "Piccola Palermo," even "Nov' Orlenza, Luigiana." To the rest of the population, white and black, it was a place to revile—"Dago Street," "Vendetta Alley." The widely read magazine *Popular Monthly* gave a typical outsider's description of an Italian tenement in New Orleans in 1891. It was described as

a ten-roomed, leaky-roofed tenement house where fifty families eat, sleep and have their being; old hags, drunken men, pale-faced young mothers and ghastly, bold-eyed children huddled together in penury and filth. A common court, the receptacle for rotten vegetables and cast-off clothing, does service as a common dressing room. A rusty pipe plays muddy water in a slime-lined basin, where sleep-begrimed eyes and crisp pink radishes are washed for the early market stalls. From this court a dozen rickety stairways lead up to as many unwholesome rooms, about whose upper galleries, out of reach of molding damp and hungry children, hang festoons of macaroni, peppers and garlic.

The Sicilians were hated by Louisiana's ruling whites who had brought them in to displace black labor. This was the third time an immigrant group was brought into New Orleans to take over the work of blacks. The second instance involved the importation of two thousand Chinese in the 1870s. The first case occurred before the Civil War, during the building of the city's canals from the two nearby large lakes, Pontchartrain and Borgne. At first black slaves were used in the construction. But their rate of death from yellow fever, malaria, typhoid, smallpox, and diphtheria caused a problem for their masters. An economic problem, not a moral one. A slave cost money. When he died, it was a loss of a capital investment for his owner. The solution came quickly to mind to the white elite. Expendable Irish immigrant laborers were brought in to replace the valuable slaves. When an Irish laborer died, the employer simply hired another Irishman, with no loss of money.

Time, the upheaval caused by the Civil War and Reconstruction, and their adaptability and talent for the city's tough politics permitted many of the English-speaking Irish-Americans (who formed 13.8 percent of the city's 1890 population) and German-Americans (15.4 percent of the population), who came in the 1840s and 1850s, to move up and share some power with the longer-established elite, composed of the Anglo-American (18.2 percent), Franco-American (17.4 percent), and Spanish-American (2.7 percent) populations.

Now, the peculiarities of the post-Reconstruction period, combined with mass emigration from Italy, made it the Sicilians' turn to be pitted against blacks—for the exploitation and degradation of both peoples. But although things at first seemed to go according to the ruling elite's plan, they were soon out of hand. The Sicilians were to become a "problem," then a threat to the same powers who first encouraged their migration to the Crescent City.

At first, Louisiana's employers, particularly the plantation owners, were delighted with the Sicilians. Labor was urgently needed. The sugar and cotton businesses were booming and rapidly expanding. Three fourths of the fertile soil of the Mississippi

Delta area had not yet been cultivated. The area's planters were competing with each other in gobbling up *three million* acres of virgin land exploitable only since 1873, when railroads opened it up.

The first profits of the economic revival were breathtaking, whetting the lust for the seemingly limitless potential wealth of the New Orleans region. In 1890, half a million people in Louisiana depended for their living on the sugar industry, which produced 330,000 hogsheads of sugar and 500,000 hogsheads of molasses per year (a hogshead equals 63 gallons). And the profits of sugar were made even sweeter that year when the U. S. Congress passed a permanent federal bonus of 1½ to 2 cents *a pound* on all sugar grown in America. There was just one apparent impediment— the black labor "problem."

There weren't enough blacks to meet the labor needs of the "New South's" economic growth. And more of the former slaves were leaving daily for the much greater economic boom of the North, or answering the call of the American West. At the same time, the southern white aristocracy was still heavily engaged in a vicious struggle to cancel the political and economic advances made by blacks during Reconstruction. Of course, the planters spoke only of the "laziness," "inefficiency," "ignorance," "thrift-lessness," and general moral and intellectual "inferiority" of blacks. After all, the South could hardly be expected to grow by remaining with "the good old Southern agricultural practice of a nigger and a mule," as John Kendall boldly put it. The suppression of blacks was masked by talk of black "sullenness" and "irresponsibility."

Italian labor seemed like a God-sent solution to replace both nigger and mule. The Sicilians worked for low wages and, in contrast to the blacks' resentment, seemed overjoyed to be able to make the little money paid them. What's more, the planters emphasized, they were far more efficient as laborers and less troublesome as people. In an 1893 letter to the Memphis *Commercial,* answering strong anti-Italian feelings which had developed by that time, a Delta plantation owner repeated the planter's early view that "the secret of the difference in favor of the Italian lay in the fact that he had laid away from the previous year everything he needed, while, as he always had done and will do, the negro raised nothing, but relied on the planter to support him. The one did as much work as possible, the other did only what constant watching compelled him to do." The appeal of the otherwise scorned Italians as plantation laborers was stressed even later by the Federal Immigration Commission. In 1909, the Commission found that under the same conditions Italians in the Delta produced 40 percent more cotton per worker than blacks, and that the "total value" produced by the Italian laborer for his employer was "85% greater" than that produced by the black worker. "Every comparison that can be drawn," the Commission concluded, "points clearly to the superiority of the Italian."

While statistics like those of the Commission were distorted by racial hatred and to mask the political suppression of the blacks, there is little doubt that the Italians were more profitable and "desirable" from the planters' point of view—but for reasons that were disastrously misunderstood.

The Sicilians who worked the sugarcane fields surrounding New Orleans closed an uncanny historical circle spanning 350 years. Sugar was first planted in Sicily by the Portuguese early in the fifteenth century. Thus, Sicilian *contadini,* or peasants, had several generations of experience in sugar growing by the time Columbus introduced cane into the New World, and more than two centuries of experience when Jesuit missionaries first brought sugar to Louisiana in 1751. Even more than experience with sugar, which most Sicilian immigrants probably did not have, their general agricultural experience was critical.

Sicilians came from an austere land where fertile soil was scarce and where farming was a constant, desperate struggle against starvation poverty. They were experts in making every square foot of land yield to its maximum possibilities.

On the other hand, Americans, both white and black, were used to wasteful practices developed in a country that seemed to be blessed with vastly more rich land than could even be worked. As a result, they were astonished at the productivity of the industrious foreigners. At first the planters seemed glad to give the Sicilians' pay to equal that of black field hands—seventy-five cents to a dollar for a working day that was twelve to sixteen hours long during planting time, and often eighteen hours long at harvest time. Moreover, during the agricultural season the Sicilians eagerly worked seven days a week in the broiling Louisiana sun, turning the soil in the spring, tending the crop in summer, and cutting with machetes the gold-green cane which turned purple in the autumn. And in the autumn, it was a rare Italian who refused to work for "overtime" wages at night in the sugar mills, grinding, cooking, boiling, and refining the product of their daytime labor. It was common for a Sicilian man, already lean when entering the United States, to lose twenty to seventy pounds in his first year in Louisiana. Many collapsed from exhaustion. Unknow numbers died, often of Louisiana's terrible tropical diseases, which were made all the more deadly by the exhaustion of the infected. In 1873, a yellow-fever epidemic killed almost one sixth of Louisiana's population. And in September 1905, *four single city blocks* in New Orleans' Italian section recorded 294 cases of yellow fever, these blocks accounting for one twelfth of the entire number of cases in the city during that year's epidemic.

The Italian laborers each earned from $30 to $45 a month during the sugar season, an unheard-of, fabulous sum by the standards of Sicily. During those evenings when they were not working in the mills, and on rainy days ("Rain=no work=no pay" was the practice of the employers), the Italians put their *contadino* skills to work on postage-stamp plots of land. The planters had laughingly agreed when the Sicilians first asked permission to cultivate these tiny plots of "useless" land for their own needs. The Sicilians called these plots *la terra benedetta* (the blessed land) and produced from them quantities of artichokes, squash, eggplants, tomatoes, celery, kale, cardoon, chicory, and strawberries that stunned the Americans. Many Italians grew enough food in these gardens to feed themselves for most of the year, making them almost independent of the exploitative "general stores" run by the planters, which kept black laborers in perpetual debt.

In 1949, Mrs. R. R. Aaronson, a Louisiana-born daughter of Sicilians, remembered some of Sicily's many sayings often repeated in the cane fields when she was a child in the 1890s. In these sayings lies the key to explaining the demon-like working patterns of the Sicilians. For example: "My house, my house, little as you are, you are to me an abbey." And the one that summed them up was simple, to the point, and absolute: "The man without family is dead."

The first Sicilians to come to Louisiana and Mississippi were working-age males—from ten years old and up. The men and boys lived crowded in one-room shacks built on stilts. Each hut had only one "window"—a glassless hole cut into a wall. They spent little on food, and lived mostly on bread and water. (Wine, a staple food for Italians, cost twenty-five cents a gallon in New Orleans, but was considered inferior by the immigrants compared with the thick wines of Sicily.) They endured a life described in their rhyme *acqua e pane, vita di cane* (water and bread, a dog's life) to send most of their money home to their families who were starving. They were resented for this last practice; the commercial and labor powers of New Orleans accused them of removing money from the city's economy. As soon as possible, money saved from the sugar-field wages bought steerage-class boat tickets for those in the old country to journey to Louisiana also.

Soon one-room huts were occupied by whole families. The males worked the fields. Females worked *la terra benedetta* and sewed clothing by hand, which, after the family's needs were met, was sold in the French Market. By 1910 the Federal Immigration Commission openly stated what had long been alarming to the plantation owners. "Where land is cheap and where opportunities for economic and social advancement are many the Italian rural laborer for wages will not outlast the first generation. . . . The Italian seems destined to become a property owner, rather than an agricultural laborer." The prospect of Italians sharing their annual 43-million-dollar (worth several times that by present-day standards) agricultural yield and their 59-million-dollar lands raised feelings considerably less than enthusiastic among Louisiana's growers. They quickly developed a determination to make sure that neither cheap land nor opportunities for economic and social advancement were to be available to the Italians.

The Sicilians were not only a threat as potential economic rivals in Louisiana; they also touched a Louisiana nerve every bit as sensitive as that of economic privilege. They were unconscionably tolerant of blacks, even friendly with them. As was true with regard to all other American ways, they showed an indifference to American racism. Coming from a land which had absorbed wave after wave of alien cultures and peoples over three thousand years, including two centuries of Arab rule, and where statues of black-skinned Madonnas were found in old churches, the Sicilians were tolerant of anybody so long as he did not threaten the one institution developed in history to insure the survival of the Sicilian people and culture. This was the complicated extended-family system from which values came and to which all responsibilities flowed. And the blacks did not threaten the Sicilian family system at all.

Both Sicilians and blacks were quick to realize the mutual benefits to be gained from commerce with each other—for example, trading Italian vegetables and clothing for possum and alligator meat gotten by black hunters. Black people (485,000 of them) outnumbered whites (455,000) in Louisiana, and to the alarm of the planters, black and Italian families even fraternized in the evenings, the Sicilians crossing over the line into the Negro quarters segregated by the plantation owners.

A new epithet was coined for Italians to go along with the American term "greenhorn" and the British-originated "dago." The whites of Louisiana now began to call these "unteachable," "uncivilized" immigrants *"black* dagoes." These new foreigners were the *only* whites to work in the fields and mills of the South's plantations. "The average white citizen," explained the Illinois Central Railroad's Industrial Commissioner, "would look upon it as an insult to work in a cotton mill. This is the situation in the large cities in the Delta. In the country the white men will not work in the field and all work is done by the negro." In fact, Italians were lumped into a separate category in Louisiana payroll lists and other records, as neither white nor black.

The status of the Italian rural workers of Louisiana was seen with a clear eye in 1905 by the Italian Ambassador to the United States. He had gone on an inspection tour of the American South, by invitation of the railroads which, still eager for Italian labor, were employing *padroni* (Judas-like Italian agents) to recruit laborers in Sicily. "The company," he wrote, much to the anger of the railroad people, "is a company of speculation. From the immigrant it tries to draw the greatest profit without caring about his well-being. The Italian is a human machine of production. Better than the Negro [in the company's eyes], a more perfect machine, but beside him a machine nevertheless."

In the winter months, when there was no work (and no wages) in the fields, the Sicilian cane workers sought work in America's cities, to return to the fields in the spring. Although a few traveled as far as Kansas City, Chicago, and New York to lay street paving stones or railroad tracks, most joined their *paesani* in New Orleans. The need there for their labor, and also to displace blacks, was as great as in the fields.

With a population of 242,000, New Orleans was by far the largest city in the South. (The second-largest, Louisville, Kentucky, had only 161,000 people.) And it was a city on the rise. The port was opened to modern ships in 1879, when jetties were completed at the mouth of the Mississippi River. A large, new industry developed almost overnight—the importation of fresh fruits from Central and South America—which was dominated by Joseph Macheca, whose stepfather pioneered it, and the business was still expanding. Whereas only 50,000 bunches of bananas entered the port in 1880, in 1887, 1,867,000 bunches came in, and by 1890 New Orleans was second only to New York as an importer of tropical fruits.

In 1883 the Southern Pacific Railroad linked the city to California. By 1890 four other lines opened it to every area of the United

States. Whereas in 1884 railroads carried 1,400,000 tons in and out of New Orleans, by 1899 they were carrying 5,500,000 tons per year. With the new rail connections, not only the New Orleans docks but its booming lumber mills hastily swallowed the cheap Italian labor in their frantic efforts to meet the building needs of the expanding American cities. Louisiana had the largest forests (22 million acres) in the South—almost untouched in 1890—50 billion feet of valuable yellow pine alone. In 1890 one New Orleans company alone (Bobet Brothers) produced four million oak staves, used throughout the United States and Europe to make casks and barrels. And the city's Louisiana Cypress Lumber Company was turning out one million shingles *a day* to meet the building needs of the incredibly expanding United States.

In addition, the fish and oyster business of Louisiana's 1,200 miles of coast was mobilized to feed the growing country. Unlike agriculture or lumber, no large capital investments were needed to catch or sell fish. Only an easily built sail-driven lugger, or a stall or pushcart nailed together from old boards. The Italians, many of them former fishermen on the island of Sicily, jumped into the business. The experienced, hard-working Sicilian fishermen and peddlers flourished against their American-born competitors— much to the annoyance and resentment of the city's commercial rulers. Recall Mayor Shakspeare's complaint in his letter to the man in Ohio that Italians "monopolize the fruit, oyster and fish trades."

In 1882, Mark Twain visited New Orleans and found it "a driving place commercially." The city's growing wealth was so magical that the $24 million debt run up by carpetbagger and black city governments before 1882 was completely paid off by the re-established white elite by 1895. By 1890, the newly arrived Italians formed a large part of the necessary labor that fueled the economic drive. But from the point of view of those who were its masters, it had become clear that the Sicilians, brought in to form a new slavery, were unmanageable and intractable. The peculiarities of the Sicilians—aloofness from outsiders and distrust of all institutions except the blood family—isolated them and made them extremely vulnerable to a deadly "solution" in the unimaginable political rats' nest of New Orleans in the "Gilded Age."

The murder of David Hennessy provided the "cover" to crush them, and may even have been planned with that in mind. A general persecution, whether one of deliberate plan, or merely one of attitude, was necessary; but not enough. Joseph Macheca, the leading symbol of Italian political power, and upward economic mobility, had to be destroyed. New Orleans' feuding political and economic interests closed ranks behind Mayor Shakspeare in the effort. Many of their motives and interests were camouflaged as they portrayed their actions as a crusade against the "Mafia."

10

If there was real fright behind the great show of fear about the Mafia in New Orleans, it was groundless. Although there was "Black Hand" extortionist activity by small bands of petty Italian criminals, including probably the Provenzano and Mantranga families, against other Italians, there is not a shred of evidence that any large or powerful Italian criminal association existed there, *at that time.* Thus, evidence had to be invented. With great fanfare, Mayor Shakspeare made public a list of "ninety-four Mafia murders" in New Orleans. He glossed over the fact that the murders took place over a period of twenty-five years. Also he did not say that the roll was put together simply by listing every homicide victim in the city with an Italian-sounding name, including some listed as "identity unknown," and also including several Spanish names because of his inability to distinguish between them. And he sloughed off the fact that ninety-one of the murders were unsolved—the police didn't know who the murderers were. The assumption that the killers were Italian, let alone Mafiosi, was pure speculation. Moreover, the three cases that were solved were cases clearly explained as non-Mafia affairs. They were murders arising out of love triangles. The nation's press failed to note any of this, and slavishly printed headlines of "Ninety-four Mafia Murders in New Orleans."

While the great Mafia scare manufactured by Shakspeare and the Committee of Fifty was baseless, the unrevealed political interests of these people in persecuting Italians was as real as their economic interests for so doing.

When Joseph A. Shakspeare was elected Mayor in 1888, he had been Mayor once before, from 1880 to 1882. At that earlier time, he was a forty-three-year-old tall, handsome man, vaguely resembling actor Gregory Peck, with a lean face, straight nose, and soft eyes. Owner of the large, profitable Shakspeare Iron Works, founded in 1845 by his father, Shakspeare was an inordinately proud and haughty individual, stiff, intensely serious and humorless—an aristocrat's aristocrat. The city's more wealthy businessmen turned to him as a new leader, a champion to fight for the privileges of New Orleans' "better class."

In his first race for office, the inexperienced Shakspeare barely won against his closest rival (9,362 votes to 8,803) in a seven-candidate, winner-take-all election. He had run as a "Reform" Democrat. "Reform" meant defeat of the regular or "Ring" element of the Democratic Party which had gained power after 1874, and which drew its great strength from the support of the city's working class. In short, reform meant restoration of complete power to the old pre-Civil War commercial aristocracy of New Orleans. This elite group was synonymous with Shakspeare's Reform wing of the Democratic Party, which with an apparent sense of humor called itself the People's Democratic Association.

But Shakspeare was to be only partially successful in this peculiar reform effort during his first term as Mayor. And his ego was to receive scars he would attempt to avenge later.

He had been the only Reform man to gain office. The several Administrators (Commissioners) elected (Finance, Police, Improvements, Accounts, Commerce, Assessments, Water Works and Public Buildings) were all Ring men. The Mayor became locked in a fight with these Ring opponents that was to consume his first term in office. It was a fight over two closely associated issues—control of the city's police and control of the city's huge gambling and prostitution business.

The "world's oldest profession" has never before or since had in America a heyday such as it had in ragtime New Orleans. Historian Herbert Asbury, in *The French Quarter,* reports that in 1899 the New Orleans police admitted to the existence of 230 bordellos, 30 houses of assignation, and about 2,000 prostitutes in the city. They ranged from the high-class (ten-dollar) whores of the plush parlor houses to ten-cent streetwalkers and fifteen-cent girls in the black bordellos known as "colored cribs." Since 1870, brothels and rooms-by-the-hour rooming houses graced nearly every block in the city. And the thickest scarlet stripe of the city was luxurious Basin Street—off limits to black and Italian "Johns." The houses there were owned by the city's elite and staffed by "fashionable hostesses" strictly for the better class. The street was "lined with the most pretentious, ostentatious, expensive brothels in the United States." Asbury wrote that they were "three-story mansions of brick and brownstone, many of them built with the aid of politicians and state and city officials, and filled with mahogany and black walnut woodwork and furniture, Oriental rugs and carpets, silver door-knobs, grand pianos, carved marble fireplaces and mantels, and copies of famous paintings and statuary."

The "sporting houses" of the city were also gambling casinos, offering every game from dice and cards to roulette. Because gambling and prostitution were illegal, it is impossible to know how much income they produced. But it is safe to say that they formed an immensely profitable business—perhaps even better than the city's leading legitimate industry, sugar.

Shakspeare and his People's Democratic Association depicted, and history books ever since have accepted, their reform cause as one of clean, honest government to put an end to the notorious corruption of the Ring. But their intent included recapturing total control of all money and power in the city, both legitimate and otherwise, which they had been forced to share after the war, first with northern carpetbaggers and blacks until 1875, and since then with "lower class" southern white elements. But the take-over had to be camouflaged.

The many scandals surrounding the sporting houses made them one of two ideal targets for the Reformers. The brothel-casinos were murderous places. Their whores and professional gamblers wielded some of the deadliest guns and knives in town, no mean distinction in New Orleans. Some of the prostitutes acted as their own bouncers, and it was said that one lady in particular could beat any man in town in a fistfight.

Every morning, the public read of the numerous sporting-house casualties from the night before in Charity Hospital's wards and morgue.

Violent crime was not the only reason for disgust. Although it was *not* true that expensive Basin Street was, as the song had it, "the place where the white and black folks meet," it certainly was true of bordellos elsewhere in town. Black and white women worked together in many houses, servicing men of both races, as well as Italian men, who were considered to be "less than white" by the other whites. (An incidental but ironic fact is that because of the strong family patterns of Sicilians, virtually none of their women ended up working in the city's bordellos, while thousands of other poor white and black girls were forced into them, usually before they were sixteen years old. As in all things, the Sicilians here too were proving troublesome to exploit.) Racial integration of vice had existed for generations in New Orleans, but it caused much concern among whites when black power became a problem after the Civil War. On May 22, 1888, the New Orleans *Lantern* noted that "in our daily walks through life we notice the surprising amount of co-habitation of white men with Negro women." On November 30, 1889, the New Orleans *Mascot* protested that "this thing of white girls becoming enamored of Negroes is becoming rather too common."

Mayor Shakspeare set about to reform things—in his fashion. He announced and implemented "the Shakspeare Plan." Acting according to this plan, he forced sixty-seven casinos to close by having the city literally extort protection money from them and harass them with goon squads of private police when they couldn't pay. The Shakspeare Plan was greeted with great approval in most of the press, which chose to ignore the fact that these luckless houses were owned by the "wrong" people. That is, they were not of Shakspeare's commercial elite. Sixteen wealthier casinos within the silk-stocking area (bordered by Camp, Chartres, St. Louis, Bourbon, Carondelet, and Gravier streets) were permitted to stay open, thereby ensuring their near monopoly over the tremendous profits of vice. No one noted that these fashionable establishments were owned mostly by the same commercial class that made up Shakspeare's Reform group. Moreover, Shakspeare announced that these sixteen casino-bordellos also were to continue to pay protection money to the city on a monthly basis. He called the practice "licensing." Part of the money was used to pay the private police who made sure the other gambling houses stayed closed.

Of course, the entire Shakspeare Plan was illegal under the laws of Louisiana and New Orleans, which prohibited gambling and prostitution. Yet, four months after it went into effect, it was approved by a New Orleans grand jury, on September 1, 1881.

The Mayor's reform of vice was successful—all of its profits now went into the right hands. He then turned his efforts to the second great reform effort of his first administration, that of the city's Police Department.

Here Shakspeare ran into stiff opposition fron the Ring, led by the Police Board. At stake in the fight for control over the department was a fortune in patronage jobs and graft income. The department was thoroughly corrupt, made up principally of political appointees with no capacity for or interest in legitimate police work. Many were habitual drunks. Some were violent criminals who terrorized the population. Needless to say, there were no Italians or blacks on the force.

The struggle between Shakspeare and the Police Board, which the Mayor was losing, climaxed over the question of who had the power to appoint and fire members of the force. The Police Board seemed to win when it created the office of Chief of Detectives and appointed Thomas Devereaux to it, over Shakspeare's veto. Only Police Administrator Patrick Mealey (a Ring man shot to death six years later by a city cop), Chief of Police Thomas N. Boylan, and Detectives David and Michael Hennessy had backed the Mayor. Yet the Mayor's defeat was soon turned around when the Hennessy cousins killed Devereaux. In historian Joy Jackson's words:

> The immediate effect of Devereaux's death upon City Hall was a complete about-face by the shocked and frightened administrators [Police Board]. Hurriedly, they met with the mayor and dissolved the office of chief of detectives. They also repealed several other recent police ordinances. . . . What had begun as a campaign to weaken Boylan [and Shakspeare] ended as a movement to give him full authority.

Although the Mayor and the Police Board were to be deadlocked until he left office in 1882, David Hennessy's bullet saved Shakspeare from complete defeat in his fight to control the department. It also earned Hennessy the hatred of Devereaux's supporters on the force, as well as the Ring. As no one noted after Hennessy's death, his killing Devereaux made him a leading partisan in the struggle between the corrupt and ruthless Ring and the Reformers, equally corrupt and ruthless despite their successful moralistic front and good press.

Shakspeare was bitter about his failure to capture the police force, as he was about other defeats. For example, he had ordered the police to close the newspaper *Mascot* by force in 1882 because it was opposing a scheme by one of his wealthy supporters to retain control of a profitable city streetcar franchise, and had printed cartoons of Shakspeare as a mule labeled "our mare." (A court injunction obtained by the paper forbade the police from carrying out the order.)

When it became clear that he could not be re-elected in 1882, Shakspeare refused to run and retired to "private affairs." These included his selling, at a good price, a two-story building on Delord Street to Mary Hines, alias Abbey Reed, whom Herbert Asbury called "the most popular prostitute in New Orleans." Shakspeare enabled the woman to go into business for herself by turning the building into "a high class assignation house."

Shakspeare's party's candidate lost badly in 1882, but the struggle continued between Reformers and the Ring, and in 1888 Shakspeare re-entered the battle and was again elected Mayor. He was intent upon taking up the fight once again to capture the Police Department, or as his campaign platform had put it, "to have the police force purged and remodeled." And one of his first moves toward this goal was to call David Hennessy back to the force as Chief. Hennessy was, then, a most conspicuous target for the many violent and corrupt policemen whose jobs he threatened, and for the Ring men who shared with them a fabulous graft income. Moreover, the department still contained many of the associates of Thomas Devereaux, whom Hennessy had killed.

Yet the Committee of Fifty ignored all of this in its "investigation" of Hennessy's murder, and concentrated solely on the persecution of Italians. With Mayor Shakspeare, it now announced that the Italian Government's Consul in New Orleans had turned over a list of "over one thousand" Italian criminal fugitives and men with criminal records who migrated from Italy to New Orleans. Once again, the country's newspapers ran banner headlines of "1,100 Dago Criminals" and "Vast Mafia in New Orleans." And once again the newspapers took little interest in the Consul's statements a few days later that, one, his list was of only *three hundred* men; two, that he had said they were criminals of all types; three, he had *not* said they were members of a criminal society; and four, he had not said they were in New Orleans. The Italian Government had believed some of these three hundred men with criminal records *might have* gone to New Orleans, then a major port of entry for Italian immigrants. Its Consul had turned over a list of their names to city officials for investigation since some of them were still wanted in Italy.

The die was cast. The nation was convinced that a Mafia conspiracy of thousands had killed Hennessy and was threatening to take over New Orleans.

11

Frustrated in its efforts to find anything incriminating against the imprisoned Italians, the Committee of Fifty hired two spies to do the job. One was a Pinkerton agent sent from New York, an experienced Italian-American detective named Francis P. Dimaio. Posing as a man named Antonio Ruggerio, the spy got himself arrested in Amite, a town about sixty miles from New Orleans, on a charge of carrying a suitcase full of counterfeit money. He was placed in Parish Prison, where, in time, he gained the confidence of the Italians charged with Hennessy's murder. These prisoners accepted him, told him many confidential things, but always maintained their complete innocence in the Hennessy affair.

Finally, the Pinkerton spy went to work on the one prisoner he found to be the weakest and most fearful. He was Emmanuele Polizzi, a laborer who had once been fired by the Provenzano brothers. Polizzi was charged with joining the Mantrangas in killing the Police Chief out of feelings of revenge against his former employers, whose cause the Chief was allegedly about to champion. The Pinkerton man noted that Polizzi was mentally unstable—he was probably, to use today's terminology, a borderline schizophrenic. He went to work on Polizzi, telling him that his food was poisoned, that someone was trying to murder him. He told him horrible stories of people he had seen die of slow poisoning. Polizzi turned sick with fear, stopped eating, and soon was out of his head. From then on, he spent most of his time babbling madly or sitting silent for hours, staring into space.

The spy learned nothing about the Hennessy case, and after three months he was removed from prison suffering from a bad case of dysentery—one of several diseases always epidemic in the dreadful Parish Prison. The Pinkerton man left New Orleans after reporting to the district attorney and other city officials. Later, great claims were made by New Orleans authorities that he had learned detailed knowledge about the Mafia, but this "knowledge" was identical to the story told by the Provenzanos to reverse their conviction.

Another spy, Thomas Collins, was employed and paid out of city funds by Mayor Shakspeare, to whom he reported directly. He was one of two New Orleans private detectives hired by the Italians' lawyers to assist them in collecting evidence for the defense. This second spy was present at meetings of the defense lawyers and their clients and had access to all the evidence the defense possessed. Through him, the district attorney knew in advance, and in complete detail, what the defense's courtroom case would be. Yet Collins learned nothing that indicated the prisoners were guilty of killing Hennessy. Again, however, great knowledge was claimed by Collins' efforts, but never specified. It is important to note that the roles played by these two spies were not made public until *several days after* the close of the Italians' trial and the events of the following day.

Meanwhile, the Italians' lawyers charged that, because of the hatred being directed against their clients as "cowardly Mafia murders of the beloved Chief Hennessy," they were being subjected to frequent beatings by the other prisoners in Parish Prison, white and black, and especially under direction by a convict leader who ran things "on the inside." The charge was corroborated by the Italian Consul, who visited the accused in prison and found several of them badly bruised and bloodied. The attorneys demanded that the nineteen Italians be removed from Parish Prison, in which they were being held without bail.

At first Mayor Shakspeare said that the charges of beatings were false. In his first statement on the charge, made on October 18, 1890, Shakspeare said:

The rumor of maltreatment of the suspects, I am satisfied is without foundation. On the contrary, I greatly fear that consideration for their personal comfort and the wishes of their friends has been carried beyond the limit of prudence.

According to standard practice in Parish Prison, wealthy prisoners could buy decent rooms there and have outside food brought in. Macheca and Mantranga availed themselves of these privileges. But the other seventeen Italian-Americans were at the mercy of the prison, its horrible conditions, and its corrupt system. In November 1890, Corte repeated his charges, now supported by lawyers hired to defend the nineteen men accused of killing Hennessy. This time the charges were denied by one of the two men in charge of prisoners, Criminal Sheriff Gabriel Villere. A grand jury investigated conditions in the prison, and on November 29, 1890, it issued its findings. They were that housing, bedding, and food in the prison were appalling, that prisoners were frequently assaulted and robbed, and that life inside the walls was run by an unnamed brutal convict leader. The report recommended that Sheriff Villere be held responsible for immediate reforms, a recommendation in which the New Orleans *Times-Democrat* had no faith. On December 8, the paper editorialized:

Mr. Villere is thus the embodiment, as well as the advocate of the existing vicious system. . . . There is, therefore, no prospect of the needed reform, or, indeed, of any reform at all, with Mr. Villere at the head of them.

The paper proved to be correct. Villere was placed in charge of reforms, and these never took place.

On the other hand, the prison's warden, Captain Lemuel Davis, admitted from the beginning that Corte's charges were true, but said he found it impossible to protect the Italians adequately in the extremely crowded, antiquated hellhole of a prison, where eight-year-old child offenders and the city's insane were mixed in with adult criminals. Warden Davis recommended that the nineteen Italians be moved elsewhere.

Shakspeare refused the request, and the Italians remained in

69

Parish Prison. In a fit of spite, he ordered that they were to have no visitors except their attorneys, not even their families. The command was partially canceled by a court order obtained by the prisoners' lawyers directing the warden to admit the Italians' families during regular visiting hours.

The drumfire of propaganda against the Italians continued, with the Mayor, the Committee of Fifty, and the press claiming every action on the part of the defense lawyers was part of a bold Mafia conspiracy to thwart justice. In fact, District Attorney Charles Luzenberg moved, unsuccessfully, to have the defense attorneys barred from the meetings in November 1890 of the grand jury hearing evidence in Hennessy's murder. (Not to be confused with the Committee of Fifty, this grand jury merely heard evidence presented to them by the district attorney and the Committee of Fifty. Two members of the grand jury were actually members of the Committee—S. P. Walmsley and Simon Hernsheim.)

12

The authorities announced that the Italians accused of Hennessy's murder would be tried in two groups. Nine of the men would go on trial first, the remaining ten to be tried separately at a later date. The first nine were Joseph Macheca; Charles Mantranga; the crazed Emmanuele Polizzi; Pietro Monasterio, the cobber living across the street from where Hennessy was shot; Monasterio's friend, Antonio Marchesi; Marchesi's fourteen-year-old son Gaspare; Antonio Scaffidi, who had partially recovered from being shot in the neck by the newspaper seller; and Bastian Incardona, the fugitive from justice in Italy.

The trial of the Italian-Americans began on February 28, 1891, in old St. Patrick's Hall. The legal cast in the trial consisted of a group of men who had a tangle of past associations with David Hennessy. The judge, Joshua G. Baker, had presided at the first trial of the Provenzano group for the shooting of the Mantranga party, during which he allowed several high-ranking policemen to give irrelevant testimony on behalf of the defendants in so suspicious a manner that it provoked a grand-jury investigation.

The district attorney who headed the prosecution, C. H. Luzenberg, was a son of the judge who had presided at Hennessy's trial and acquittal for the murder of Devereaux. The D.A. had been party to the activities of Shakspeare's spy, Thomas Collins, which included sitting in on the defendants' conferences with their lawyers. He was assisted in the prosecution by two prominent lawyers who had been defense lawyers for the Provenzanos during their second trial. One of them had also defended Hennessy in the Devereaux murder trial.

The defense lawyers included two well-known attorneys,

Thomas J. Semmes, a former attorney general of Louisiana and former Confederate senator, and Lionel Adams, a former district attorney of New Orleans. Their services were paid for mostly with Joseph Macheca's and Charles Mantranga's money. Adams had defended Hennessy in the Devereaux trial, and prosecuted the Provenzanos in their two trials. Semmes had also prosecuted the Provenzanos.

No one took note that this confusing web of personal associations and possible conflicts of interest might jeopardize chances for a fair trial. The press, on the other hand, gave front-page play to rumors that the prestigious defense lawyers had been hired with "Mafia money," and that the defense employed a man named Dominick O'Malley, in addition to Shakspeare's spy, to help prepare its case. O'Malley was the private detective who had been ejected from the courtroom during the first Provenzano trial upon a complaint by the Provenzanos' lawyers that he was trying to signal to a juror. Like most New Orleans private detectives, O'Malley was tough, unscrupulous, and operated by the unethical, crude standards of the city. From the beginning, newspapers printed unsubstantiated rumors that he was out to bribe the jury on behalf of the Italian defendants.

Prosecution and defense lawyers first sparred with each other in the selection of a jury. Each side had what amounted to unlimited privilege to reject jury candidates. Hundreds of candidates were rejected by the defense because they admitted they were prejudiced against Italians or would not give any credence to Italian witnesses. After the examination of 780 potential jurors, twelve men were selected who satisfied both sides. (The names and occupations of the jurors are in Appendix H.)

The atmosphere in the court during jury selection can be seen in a local newspaper's account of one jury candidate, "a Hebrew," who was laughed at by the spectators when he "as is the strict custom of his race, put his hat on his head."

Of course, the prosecution permitted no one of Italian background to serve on the jury.

The trial lasted two weeks. The state called sixty-seven

witnesses, and the defense called eighty-four. One of the key witnesses was Zachary Foster, the black laborer arrested running from the murder scene. He swore that *although there was a uniformed Boylan policeman on the street at the time,* he saw four men fire at Hennessy. He said that Monasterio, Scaffidi, the senior Marchesi, and Polizzi "looked pretty like" them.

Emma Thomas, the black woman who lived near Monasterio's room, told her story of going out several moments after hearing the gunfire and seeing Monasterio standing on the sidewalk, empty-handed, barefoot, and wearing only his underclothes, and the Italian shouting to her, "Emma, Emma! The Chief, the Chief, mamma's shoes!"

Mary Wheeler, who had identified Scaffidi as one of Hennessy's murderers in the dubious cell-block tour on the morning after the shooting, now could not identify the man in court.

Another black laborer, James T. Poole, swore he had been walking home, from a bar, behind Hennessy and saw four or five men shoot him. He said two of them were the elder Marchesi and Scaffidi, the latter of whom he described as wearing a yellow oilskin coat. Upon being shown the oilskin coat taken from Scaffidi's fruit stand, the witness said it was not the one—it was black.

A bartender named John B. Daure swore that he ran to the murder scene upon hearing shots and saw Scaffidi, the senior Marchesi, and Antonio Bagnetto, all of whom he knew personally. He testified that all three had guns in their hands and that he saw Scaffidi actually fire his. He also swore he saw Marchesi's son, whom he knew, running from the scene. Upon cross-examination, the witness admitted knowing the Acting Chief of Police and speaking to him "frequently" about the case.

Mr. F. Peeler testified that he went to the second-story balcony of his house when awakened by gunfire and saw Scaffidi firing and Bagnetto standing nearby. He also saw a uniformed Boylan policeman at the scene. Later a reporter for the New Orleans *Times-Democrat* testified that he interviewed Peeler shortly after the

nooting, and that he was "incoherently drunk," and that Mrs. eeler said he had been drunk since hours before the shooting.

A laborer swore he saw Polizzi running from the scene after hots were fired.

The lumberyard watchman swore he saw three men walking fast ear the scene of the shooting. He asked them what happened, nd said that one answered, "Me no knowee." The men, who he hought were Italians, then ran. The watchman then met two more nen, one with a gun. Upon his asking them, "What's that you've ot?" they ran without answering. He identified them as Polizzi nd Scaffidi. He also identified two of the ten other Italians who vere awaiting a later trial as being two of the three men he first aw.

A black teen-ager swore that the teen-age Marchesi confessed o him that he had been lookout for the Chief and marked him by vhistling to the gunmen when he saw him coming. The teen-ager ast doubt on his testimony by adding that young Marchesi told iim, "I have turned State's evidence against my father. I have wined my father up." In fact, he had *not* turned state's evidence.

A woman who owned the shanty in which Monasterio lived wore that Joseph Macheca, calling himself Peter Johnson, per-onally rented it "for a friend" three months before Hennessy was ,hot, and later it was occupied by Monasterio. However, this voman had not been party to the alleged transaction, and the voman whom she named as the one who dealt with Macheca vas not called to testify.

Throughout the trial, Italian spectators in the courtroom were .reated with hostility, contempt, or ignorant condescension. An example of the latter is seen in a "sympathetic" description of Scaffidi's sister given in the *New Delta* on March 7:

Among those in court prominent for her size and beauty was a young Italian woman. She was a typical daughter of sunny Italy. She was truly beautiful—her beauty was of the Junoesque type. Although not over 24 years of age, yet her weight was over 200 pounds. Her dress was elegant and she wore a large quantity of jew-

elry. In her ears were the large earrings for which Sicilians are proverbial. Although in the morning nothing of interest took place, still this beautiful young woman was all excitement, and spoke continually to two old women who were her companions. Her large black eyes scanned the entire building, and everyone that entered the courtroom was stared at by her with a wild, hunted look. . . . It is said that her love for her unfortunate brother is phenomenal, and that she doubts the idea of her brother being a murderer, and asserts her belief in his entire innocence.

On the third day of the trial, the "wild" image of the Italians was reinforced when Emmanuele Polizzi, who had been staring into space until then, suddenly became very excited and started shouting in Italian. Through an interpreter, it was learned that he was raving about not wanting to die and wanting to confess. The prisoner was taken into the judge's chambers, with lawyers from both sides. After fifteen minutes, all returned to the court and the judge and district attorney said Polizzi's confession was "worthless" ranting, not to be entered in evidence. Given a new lawyer, Polizzi was seated off by himself, and once again fell into a blind gaze. Five days later he erupted again. This time he threw his arms about and shouted wildly. He tried to jump through a window, cutting himself. It took a dozen guards to subdue the short, slight Italian. Dragged to another room, he there said, according to what police told reporters, that Joseph Macheca and Charles Mantranga were heads of the Mafia, which "was under the protection of St. Joseph," and that the judge and jury would suffer vengeance —something which never happened. Newspaper accounts of this "confession" caused a sensation the next day. When returned to the courtroom, Polizzi again went wild and it took a prolonged fight by eight guards to subdue the handcuffed man. The judge ordered a sanity hearing for him. *That day,* he was found sane, and was returned to court the next morning in chains. He spent the day trying to bite people who walked near him in the courtroom.

In his summation, the district attorney alleged that Joseph Macheca headed a conspiracy to kill Hennessy, and that the other

accused carried out the ambush when the Chief was "fingered" by the whistle of young Marchesi.

As the defense opened its case, the legendary prizefighter John L. Sullivan caused the trial to be interrupted by entering the courtroom. Court officials set up a special chair just to the right of the jury box for the distinguished spectator, giving the jurors the distinct impression that their decision upon the killers of a great Irish police chief would have to stand the scrutiny of the great Irish boxer. The effect was cemented by John L.'s friendly hello to the Attorney General of Louisiana, who was sitting at the prosecution table as an "observer"—giving the jury the impression that the state's popular Governor wanted a "guilty" verdict.

On the morning the defense was to open its case, the city police arrested the defense assistant, private detective Dominick O'Malley, on a charge of carrying a weapon. Rumors increased throughout the city that O'Malley was trying to bribe the jury.

The defense hit the alleged motive for the defendants' murdering Hennessy by calling Captain A. Kalinski, a policeman and friend of Hennessy since the two men were boys. Kalinski swore that Hennessy told him that he knew nothing about the Provenzano-Mantranga shooting and that he would not have any testimony to give at the Provenzanos' second trial.

Four men, none of them Italian, each testified they separately saw Antonio Bagnetto at his fruit stand in the Poydras Market at the time of the murder.

Antonio Scaffidi's sister and an Italian midwife testified that he was with them at the time of the killing tending Scaffidi's wife, who had a miscarriage that night.

An Italian woman named Iania Roma testified she lived with Polizzi and that he was in bed with her at the time of the assassination.

A large number of Italian and non-Italian witnesses swore that Joseph Macheca and Charles Mantranga were at a theater at the time of the murder.

The trial ended on March 12. Judge Baker instructed the jury to find Charles Mantranga and Bastian Incardona "not guilty" because no evidence at all had been offered against them. The jury then retired to consider the case against the others.

The next afternoon it returned and handed Judge Baker the verdict. The judge stared at it in silence for several minutes, in what spectators thought to be disapproval, then had it read aloud. The jury could not agree on a verdict for Polizzi, Monasterio, and Scaffidi and declared a mistrial for the three men. But its verdict on the other six men was "not guilty."

The spectators in the court were stunned for a few seconds, and soon began shouting. Judge Baker quieted them, and then gave an order which was to doom the lives of most of the prisoners. He instructed that all nineteen Italians, including the six just acquitted, be returned to Parish Prison. His stated reason was not, as was later claimed, to protect the Italians, but that another charge was still pending against them—that of "lying in wait with intent to commit the murder" of Hennessy. This charge against the six men just acquitted of Hennessy's death was, of course, absurd.

By this time, the crowd outside the courthouse was shouting angrily and pushing against police lines. The Italian prisoners were hurried out a side entrance of the building by a squad of sheriff's deputies and taken back to Parish Prison. The jurors were escorted through the crowd by another squad of deputies, and were greeted by shouts of "How much did you get?" and other insults. While still in the courtroom, District Attorney Luzenberg announced to the press that he would investigate rumors that the jury had been "bribed with one hundred thousand dollars."

The next morning, March 14, the newspapers of New Orleans carried an advertisement which sent shock waves through the Italian community:

MASS MEETING

All good citizens are invited to attend a mass meeting on Saturday, March 14, at 10 o'clock A.M., at Clay Statue, to take steps to remedy the failure of justice in the Hennessy case.

Come prepared for action.

77

13

In the early morning, Pasquale Corte, the Italian Consul in New Orleans, saw the newspaper ad calling for a mass meeting. Vigorous and diligent in his job, he immediately set out to stop the coming bloodbath. Although his relations with the city authorities had once been good, they had cooled considerably since he corrected their lies about his list of Italian fugitives. Since then, his protests against the beatings of the imprisoned Italians and abuse of the general Italian population had put him in direct confrontation with Mayor Shakspeare and the Committee of Fifty. His alarm about the ad was heightened by the long list of those who signed it. Among the sixty-one signers were the names of Shakspeare's right-hand man, Reformer William S. Parkerson, and several members of the Committee of Fifty. They included the Committee's first chairman, Edgar H. Farrar; and the editor of the *New Delta,* John C. Wickliffe, a thirty-seven-year-old grandson of a man who had been Governor of Kentucky, U.S. congressman, and U. S. Postmaster General, and a nephew of a former Governor of Louisiana. As a young man, John Wickliffe had been thrown out of West Point on disciplinary grounds. Among the other Committee of Fifty members who signed the ad were Walter D. Denegre, a wealthy lawyer and property owner, and Ring political boss James D. Houston. (See Appendix I for a full list of those who signed the ad.)

Consul Corte recognized that the ad was, in effect, a thinly coded message that the violent White League had been revived, bringing together the city's rival political factions for a war against the Italians. The inclusion of men like Houston left little doubt about the reason for the "mass meeting." His long record of vio-

78

lence had climaxed on December 14, 1883, when he led a group of Ring politicians in a shoot-out against a bunch of Reformers. Three men died and eight were wounded in the fight. On January 12, 1885, Houston and City Sheriff Robert Brewster tried to horsewhip the editor of the *Mascot* for publishing an article uncomplimentary to Houston's brother, a judge. In the ensuing fight, Brewster was shot to death.

Corte set off in a hurry for Shakspeare's office. There, he met Louisiana Attorney General Rogers and Sheriff Villere. The Mayor's staff told them that he had not come in that morning and they did not know where he was. The Italian had them telephone Shakspeare's home, only to learn that he had left earlier for a breakfast appointment. His household did not know where or with whom. Precious time passed as the staff telephoned different places in the city looking without success for the Mayor. Corte glanced at his pocket watch. It was now after nine, less than an hour before the mob was to gather. He ran out of City Hall, jumped into a carriage, and together with Rogers and Villere sped through the streets toward a house on the outskirts of town where the Governor of Louisiana was a house guest.

The morning of March 14 was bright and sunny, and a crowd had formed early around the statue of Henry Clay, then located at Canal and Royal streets. By ten o'clock, it numbered from six to eight thousand people and was growing by hundreds every few minutes. At 10:05, Parkerson, Denegre, and Wickliffe climbed to the top of the statue's tall pedestal. Parkerson raised his hands and the crowds quieted. He was an imposing figure, thirty-four years old, six feet tall and well built, with a full brown mustache. His dark, intense eyes were "snapping fire" as he gazed at the crowd, according to witnesses. His voice, described as usually soft and caressing, was untypically firm and strong as he denounced the "infamous jury" that had acquitted the "Mafia Society" the day before. He then got to the business of the day. "Will every man here follow me, and see the murder of D. C. Hennessy vindicated?" (Parkerson's full speech is given in Appendix J.) The crowd went mad, shouting, "Yes, yes, hang the dagoes!" Next it was Denegre's turn to harangue the crowd, followed by Wickliffe, "tall, stalwart and of *distingué* appearance," whose last words were: "Gentlemen, let's go and do our duty. Mr. Parkerson is your leader. Mr. Houston is your first lieutenant. Your second lieutenant is myself."

The three men led the mob through the streets toward Parish Prison. The crowd had a festive air about it as "the fairest and bravest of Southern women" in windows along the way "raised their hands aloft and waved snow white handkerchiefs at the passing army." At the corner of Royal and Bienville streets, they were joined by seventy to one hundred men armed with Winchester repeating rifles and shotguns who placed themselves at the head of the mob. This was an "execution squad." It had all been privately arranged the evening before, first at a meeting of about thirty men, made up from the Reform group, at Parkerson's law office just two hours after the jury had returned its verdict, and then in a second, larger meeting of both Reform and Ring men, those who signed the newspaper ad, later that night at the home of Frank B. Hayne on Bienville Street. After the second meeting, the conspirators took 150 repeating rifles from the A. Baldwin and Company warehouse and brought them to Hayne's home for use the next day by the execution squad.

As the mob entered the Negro neighborhood which surrounded Parish Prison, a reporter heard an old black woman say, "Thank God it wasn't a nigger who killed the Chief!"

People in the mob spoke indignantly about the "Mafia celebration" the night before in "Dago Alley." March 14 was the birthday of Italy's reigning King, Umberto I. As was their annual custom, the Sicilians had planned a *festa* on Decatur Street. They had decorated the street for the celebration. The rest of the city became overwrought by rumors about the "Mafia flag" being in the streets. Actually, these were miniatures of Italy's old royal flag which had been strung along streetlamps for the festival.

Consul Corte found Governor Francis T. Nicholls at the breakfast table. Nicholls, an archetypal southern patriarch with white hair and a "Kentucky colonel" beard, was in fact a former Confederate brigadier general who had lost an arm at Winchester, and returned to combat duty and lost a foot at Chancellorsville. Icy and fearless, he was greatly admired in Louisiana for his role in ending Reconstruction in the state. In January 1877, he had led three thousand White Leaguers who drove at gunpoint the Reconstructionists out of the state government buildings and out of the government itself. He had then had himself sworn in as Governor after he *lost* a much-contested election to a Reconstructionist Republican.

Nicholls, a friend of Mayor Shakspeare, listened attentively as the Italian urged that he intervene to stop mob action. He replied that he had seen the ad, but was convinced there was no danger of violence at what would be a "peaceful meeting." In any case, he said, he could not interfere in city affairs unless he was asked to do so by New Orleans officials. He reassured the Italian by saying that he had called the Pickwick Club, where he knew Shakspeare was to have breakfast, and left a message for him to return the call. Nicholls suggested that the Consul wait with him for the call, and have some breakfast in the meantime. Corte declined breakfast and sat tense and silent as the Governor went on eating and chatted amiably about other matters. The Italian glanced at his watch. It was now several minutes after ten.

The mob, which now numbered from twelve to twenty thousand people, crowded around and in Congo Square (since renamed Beauregard Square), next to where the prison stood. The prison was surrounded, and all streets leading to the area were clogged by the large crowd. Congo Square, which got its name because of the blacks who lived there and danced "African style" in the square (in 1891 doing a popular dance called the "hog face"), much to the entertainment of tourists, was bordered by ramshackle buildings housing poor blacks. In their desire for the mob to be seen as "all New Orleans" by the watching world, its leaders invited blacks to join it, and many did.

Inside the prison, Warden Davis had issued modern repeating rifles to his guards and positioned them inside the institution's two gates with orders to defend the building. Earlier in the morning, he had been alarmed when ten city policemen on duty outside the main gate left and did not return. He tried several times to reach the Mayor on the telephone, without success. He talked with Sheriff Villere, who went off, the latter said, to search for the Governor and the Attorney General of the state.

Davis went down to the main gate at Orleans Street to speak with the leaders of the mob. Shouting to him through the massive bars of the large gate, Parkerson and the others demanded that he open the prison and turn the Italians over to them. Davis refused, and went back inside the building.

The mob was furious. They tried to force the main gate with crowbars, picks, and sledgehammers, but with no effect at all on the massive door made entirely of steel. Then someone remembered that the prison had another gate, on Treme Street. This one was much smaller, and made mostly of oak wood. The mob turned its efforts on this gate. Using railroad ties found at a nearby street construction site, teams of racially mixed men began battering the gate.

Davis sent most of his guards to the Treme Street gate and ordered them to shore it from inside with timbers, while he tried frantically to reach the Mayor and the city's Police Chief on the telephone. He could not contact them. Finally, realizing that the Treme Street gate would be forced, he ordered all prisoners locked in their cells, except the Italians. He assembled these nineteen men, and with the sounds of the battering rams booming in their ears, told them he could not hold the prison much longer. He informed them he was turning them free within the prison to hide themselves as best they could, and suggested the women's section as a hiding place. The Italians pleaded with him for guns to defend themselves. Davis refused. He told them he would give them a few minutes to hide and then would lock all the gates inside the prison to obstruct the mob when it got inside. The nineteen prisoners scrambled throughout the large building.

After what seemed an interminable time to Corte, the telephone rang. Attorney General Rogers answered it, listened for a moment, then hung up. He turned to Corte and Nicholls and told them that a mob had marched to Parish Prison and was now inside it. The Consul bolted from the house and raced his carriage toward Parish Prison, intent on defending the prisoners himself. He had no idea of the number of people surrounding it.

The gate at Treme Street was badly smashed and hanging by splinters. The attackers paused for a moment, grouped a team of men led by an enormous black man carrying a huge stone in front of him, and charged the gate. Its doors flew apart, and the mob was inside. The guards in the courtyard inside the gate made no effort to resist, and in fact some turned their rifles over to the mob leaders when they entered.

Parkerson, Wickliffe, and Houston gathered about sixty of the specially armed execution squad inside the prison. The rest of the squad stayed at the gate, blocking entrance to the mob. Each of the three leaders took a team of about twenty men and went hunting for the Italians, over the protests of Warden Davis, who was simply pushed aside.

One squad, having been told by some guards of Davis' recommendation to the Italians to hide in the women's section, headed up the stairs to the third story, where the women's cells were located. Six Italians were in the corridor there, including Monasterio. When they heard the squad coming up the steps, they ran to the other end of the floor and down another stairway to an outdoor yard.

The gates to the yard were locked; the men were trapped. In a moment their pursuers burst into the yard, having been told by the women prisoners where the Italians had gone. The Italians clustered together at one end of the yard and the squad opened fire from about twenty feet away. More than a hundred rifle shots and shotgun blasts were fired into the six men, tearing their bodies apart. When the firing stopped, the squad inspected their victims. A man saw Monasterio's hand twitch and yelled, "Hey, this one's still alive!" "Give him another load," another gunman answered. "Can't, I ain't got the heart." Then one of the men walked up to the body, aimed a shotgun point-blank, and literally blew the top of Monasterio's head away. Someone laughed. There were two or three cheers. One or two men turned their faces away, looking sick.

Meanwhile, another group of self-appointed executioners chased Macheca, Scaffidi, and the elder Marchesi through an upper corridor of the male section, and cornered them, appropriately, in a large gallery for condemned men. The three Italians turned to face their pursuers. Macheca had picked up an Indian club to defend himself. Before he could raise it, several of the attackers fired from the corridor just a few feet from them through the bars of a window opening onto the gallery. One of the first bullets hit Macheca in the head, knocking him backward. As Scaffidi looked at him, lying dead with the club still clutched in his hand, he was hit by a shotgun blast which entered his right eye and tore away half of his head. As he fell backward, he raised his right arm, "as if to strike, while his left arm was forward as a guard."

Marchesi was struck in the head by a bullet. As he raised his right hand to shield himself, a shotgun charge blew it off and went on to disintegrate the top of his skull. Yet he did not die until nine hours later, lying all the time where he fell.

The gunmen were frustrated at having to search for the hidden Italians, and began to tear things apart looking for them. They discovered Polizzi sitting on the floor in a corner of a cell, muttering to himself. Four or five men dragged him into a corridor. He stood before them, staring with wild eyes at nothing in particular, and was shot two or three times. Bagnetto was found in another cell, pretending to be dead. He too was shot.

Hearing the shots from within the prison, the crowd outside was going wild with blood lust, demanding to be let in on the kill. Parkerson, Wickliffe, Denegre, and Houston held a quick conference within a prison corridor. The mob was becoming unmanageable, and the last thing they wanted was a general riot. They held vivid memories of federal troops entering the city to restore order during riots just a few short years past during the Reconstruction period—for example, in 1874 when President Grant sent troops and three warships to crush a White League attack against the Metropolitan Police. Federal troops would mean the disruption of everything the lynch leaders desired for themselves as *de facto* rulers of the city. Although they had been in the prison less than twenty minutes, and had not yet found eight of the nineteen Italians, they made a quick decision. They would allow the mob to spend its frenzy for blood on the men already shot, and then Parkerson would attempt to disperse the crowd.

They selected first the Italian who had caused the most public sensation at the trial which ended the day before. They ordered that Polizzi, who was still breathing, be carried out to the crowd. The mob went mad at the sight of the semi-conscious Italian, "his long black hair disheveled, his naturally idiotic look intensified by the fear he had experienced." He was tossed around above the heads of the mob for a length of a block until he reached the corner of St. Ann Street. There, a rope was strung over the top bar of a streetlamp, and its noose placed around Polizzi's neck. The Italian's hands were tied in front of him, and a dozen men pulled the other end of the hangman's line, hoisting him into the air. The noise of the crowd sounded like the legions of hell. Suddenly the roar turned to an unearthly gasp as Polizzi came to and began to pull himself up the rope toward the top of the lamp. After several seconds as the man tried to climb for his life, a dozen men with rifles and pistols began shooting up at him. The mob shouted obscenities and insults as the bullets "sped upon their mission of death and the swinging body gave one final throb of stricken agony."

The crowd was pleased as gunmen continued to riddle Polizzi's body with bullets, but soon turned to the prison again, demanding more victims. This time Parkerson ordered that Bagnetto be sent out, since he was apparently not yet dead. The mob repeated its performance in tossing the limp man about and then proceeded to hang him, this time from the limb of a tree. As Bagnetto was raised by the neck, the noose slipped over his head, and "he fell in a heap upon the ground." A newsman wrote:

> It was a most horrible fall and a groan and a yell burst from the thousands looking on. The noose was placed securely around Bagnetto's neck and carefully adjusted, and with a yell and a cheer from the crowd three negroes and half a dozen white men swung the murderer as high as the fork of the limb would permit. Not a kick, motion, or squirm did he make.

Several men in the crowd used the hanging body for target practice.

William Parkerson now emerged from the prison to the ecstatic cheers of the mob, who raised him on their shoulders. Finally he mounted an overturned streetcar in Congo Square to address his followers. He began by announcing the names of the Italians killed, pausing after each because of a deafening roar from the mob which went out in waves through the people jamming the streets leading into the square as his words were shouted back by relayers in the crowd. The mob then shouted for Dominick O'Malley, who, unknown to them, had fled the city early in the morning when he saw the ad calling for mob action. Parkerson answered:

> I pledge that O'Malley will be dealt with. Now take my word for it. Mob violence is the most terrible thing on the face of the earth. I called you together for a duty. You have performed that duty. Now go to your homes and if I need you, I will call you. Now, go home and God bless you.

The crowd roared, "God bless you, Mr. Parkerson." They lifted him upon their shoulders again and marched off to carry him in triumph through the city.

Just then, Consul Corte reined in his horse as he met a wall of people clogging one of the streets approaching Congo Square. He stood high in his carriage, looked over the heads of the mob, and to his horror, saw the blood-covered hanging bodies. He went back to the Consulate, where he was harassed and threatened by thugs, as he explained in a letter to his superior describing what had happened that day. (The letter is reprinted in Appendix K.)

Thousands of people remained around the prison after Parkerson had been carried off, and they clamored to be let in to see the results of their efforts. Houston and Wickliffe arranged to have some of the bodies lined up in one large room and for the mob to be let through in a long line to view them. Thousands of people, including an estimated 2,500 women and children, streamed through for five hours. The bodies of Polizzi and Bagnetto were left hanging for two hours for viewing. Some of the women of the city came and dipped their lace handkerchiefs in their blood as souvenirs, and crowds of souvenir hunters stripped the bark from the trunk of the tree on which Bagnetto was hanging.

Meanwhile, Warden Davis searched the prison for the Italians who had escaped the mob. He found Gaspare Marchesi and brought the sobbing boy to his office, crowded with reporters and members of the mob. There, he told him of his father's fate, whereupon one man said to him in reference to his alleged role in Hennessy's murder, "I reckon you won't do any more whistling, boy." The boy turned and screamed, "I am innocent! I swear to God I was home that night, and my father was with me!" Davis attempted to throw the crowd out of his office, without success. They continued to badger the boy with questions until a doctor, summoned by Davis, knocked him out with a sedative.

Eleven Italians had been killed. (Their names are in Appendix E.) Of these, three had been acquitted the day before, three had seen the same trial result in a mistrial for them as the jury could not reach a verdict about them, and five had not been tried at all. Eight men had escaped by hiding themselves well. They included, in addition to young Marchesi, two other men acquitted the day before, Bastian Incardona, who had hid himself under a mattress in a cell, and Charles Mantranga, who with another Italian had hid himself under the floorboards in a rubbish closet in the women's section.

That night there were celebrations in New Orleans' many bars. After Hennessy's death, a local balladeer had made up a song, which became popular, about "the brave Chief Hennessy and how he met his fate" and the accused Italians, "Satanic fiends for which there should be no place but Hell." After the lynching, he penned another ballad, which was sung in New Orleans during the next decades:

> Now we have shown our Southern blood—for
> nowhere will you find—
> A Town that would have justice and fair
> play of this kind.
> We would not have the verdict given by
> them men of nerve;
> It seems to us as if the case had quite a
> crooked curve.
> The execution was gone through quickly, and
> done by gentlemen,
> And everybody will agree it could never
> be a sin.

14

Secretary of State James G. Blaine sat alone in his Washington office on the afternoon of March 14. He was tired and solemn as he read accounts of the day's lynchings. Idolized in the North for his vocal advocacy of punishing the former Confederate states, a practice he began in 1876 to draw attention away from corruption in the Republican Party's administration under President Grant, "Blaine of Maine" was a legendary orator and was immensely popular. But his thirty years in Washington were involved with repeated scandals. The "plumed knight" of the Republican Party had run for the presidency in 1884, after long playing the role of kingmaker of Republican Presidents in the United States Senate. He immediately became the focus of scandals. Conclusive evidence was produced showing that, as the Republican congressional leader, Blaine secretly used his influence and acted as a broker selling bonds of the Little Rock and Fort Smith Railroad, which immediately went bankrupt. He made $100,000 on the deal. A business letter from Blaine surfaced which proved his guilt, and which he had ended with the sentence, "Burn this letter." In addition, it was shown that he was responsible for a dubious payment to one of his friends in a diplomatic settlement with Chile while he, Blaine, had been Secretary of State under Presidents Garfield and Arthur. Moreover, Blaine was caught in lies because he had denied these charges.

At rallies, Blaine's opponents chanted:

> Blaine, Blaine, James G. Blaine
> The continental liar from the
> State of Maine.
> Burn this letter!

Blaine's forces retaliated with a chant of their own, directed at his Democratic opponent, Grover Cleveland, who had admitted to fathering an illegitimate child by a wealthy woman:

> Ma! Ma! Where's my pa?
> Gone to the White House,
> Ha! Ha! Ha!

Unable to stomach Blaine's corruption, the reform or Mugwump wing of his own party, led by Carl Schurz and George William Curtis, had bolted from the convention that nominated him, and promised support to any honest man the Democrats might put forward.

But in the end, it was another scandal, an ethnic one, which cost Blaine the election. In an election-eve rally in New York City, a Presbyterian minister, in introducing Blaine, called the Democrats the party of "Rum, Romanism and Rebellion." The anti-Catholic slur cost Blaine the city's Irish votes. These cost him New York State's electoral votes, which in turn cost him the close election.

Charles Edward Russell, Blaine's biographer, ended his book on him by saying the very popular man lacked both courage and integrity throughout his fantastic career, and was consumed by careerist ambitions. After noting his extraordinary intelligence, eloquence, wide knowledge, and impressive personal presence with his white hair and full beard ending in an inverted "V" two inches below his chin, Russell went on:

> Infinitely more impressive and more pathetic is this, that he failed to leave anything but the record of an almost incredible popularity starting with little and ending in naught. . . . No other man in our annals has filled so large a space and left it so empty.

Historians Samuel Eliot Morison and Henry Steele Commager echo the judgment in their *Growth of the American Republic:*

"Aside from his personality he made no impression upon American politics except to lower its moral tone."

Yet, as his detractors admit, Blaine was a politician's politician, a wheeler-dealer unmatched in his day. But even in this, he had a great flaw as Secretary of State. As one of his friends put it, it was his "failure in tact as a diplomatist." He tended to carry over his behavior as congressional back-room deal maker and party hatchet man. This tendency was complicated in 1891 by his poor health. A lifelong hypochondriac, he was now morbid about his sickness. Once flamboyant, his emotions were now often brittle and his manner often irritable and cutting. He was also bitter about the failures of his political ambitions, and the death in the last fifteen months of two of his six children, his favorite son, Walker, and his daughter Alice.

While he was reading of the morning's lynchings in New Orleans, a secretary interrupted him to inform him that the Italian Ambassador was there to see him.

The Ambassador, Baron Francesco Severio Fava, was an Italian nobleman of the Old World. The fifty-nine-year-old Fava was a descendant of one of the "oldest" families of Naples. He was a highly experienced career diplomat, having served his country in Switzerland, Holland, Turkey, Romania (where he helped ease the condition of the persecuted Jews of that country), and as Ambassador to Argentina. He had been Ambassador to the United States for nine years, and he and his urbane wife spoke flawless English. The Favas were well integrated into Washington life, where their thirty-year-old son was a well-known civil engineer. They were well liked and respected in the city. This afternoon the Ambassador showed none of the charm that usually took the edge off his extreme formality. He sat rigid and aggressive in his customary extra-high starched collar, gazing through his lorgnette, "half crazed over the tragedy" as Blaine later described him to the President. He protested the lynchings in sharp language, and asked that the President contact the Governor of Louisiana to protect the Italians there from any more violence.

After a perfunctory expression of horror over the incident,

Blaine said he would wait until the next day before he spoke to the President in order to assemble more facts than the "inexact information now at hand." The Ambassador was affronted at what he perceived as Blaine's indifferent manner. He rose, nodded stiffly, and left.

The next day Blaine received a note from President Benjamin Harrison in which the President termed the lynchings "very appalling," and said that although the federal government could not interfere in the internal affairs of a state, it could appeal to the state's authorities for proper action. Harrison was typically steady and legalistic, a contrast to his volatile Secretary of State and the angry Italian Ambassador. Blaine dutifully drafted a telegram to Louisiana Governor Nicholls reflecting the President's position. He reminded Nicholls that Italy and the United States had signed a treaty on February 26, 1871, in which the governments mutually pledged to protect the other's people living in or traveling through its territory, according to the laws of the host country. Blaine urged Nicholls to protect the Italians in his state from further harm. He also urged that he act so "that all offenders against the law may be promptly brought to justice." Blaine made a point of showing a copy of the telegram to Ambassador Fava as proof of the President's concern.

Governor Nicholls replied the next day in a telegram that was a polite but definite rebuff of the President's involvement in his state's affairs. He told Blaine that all was now quiet in New Orleans, and that the mob action had been directed only against the victims as individuals and not against the Italian "race." The Ambassador was not satisfied by Nicholls' answer, a copy of which Blaine sent to him. Fava sent to Blaine reports from Consul Corte in New Orleans asserting that the Italians there were in great fear, many of them fleeing the city—some seven hundred left by train alone in the days after the lynchings, according to railroad ticket agents. The only positive response in the reply from Nicholls was an assurance that a grand jury would meet the next day to begin an investigation of the lynchings, and presumably to hand up indictments.

After receiving a copy of Nicholls' answer, Ambassador Fava once again came to see Blaine. This time he was not merely angry but also hard. He communicated a curt official message from his government. It consisted of two demands made upon the American Government: (1) that President Harrison agree in principle that a cash indemnity should be paid by Washington to the families of the eleven lynched Italians, and (2) that the President assure Italy that all those guilty of the lynching would be punished. Blaine was annoyed at the Italian's directness. He lost his temper and began to lecture Fava acerbically on the American constitutional system, which, he said, left criminal matters entirely in the hands of state authorities. He told him that President Harrison would take no further action until the New Orleans grand jury completed its work. Again the two officials were at loggerheads, and the Ambassador left with a display of indignation.

Several days went by as each government reiterated its position to the other, mostly through quarrelsome statements in the press.

Meanwhile, the pressure upon the Italian Government from its own people was becoming irresistible. The Italian Premier, Marchese Antonio di Starabba Rudini, himself a Sicilian, was riding on a sea of public outrage. He was faced on all sides with demands that he redeem Italy's honor by seeing that the lynchers were punished. Even before the lynchings, Premier Rudini had been in trouble with his own Parliament because of charges that he was vacillating and indecisive in the face of Italy's serious economic and political problems, especially in an arms race and quasi cold war with France and Austria. Now he had to appear strong in response to the furious protests in Parliament about the lynchings. The Premier cabled his agent in Washington to press home his two demands upon the Americans with an ultimatum. Following this order, the Ambassador once again met with Blaine, on March 25. Blaine was tired and felt pressured. Fava felt equally pressured. A cross, tense discussion took place.

Fava began by saying that Consul Corte reported that at least four of the men lynched were Italian subjects. Blaine argued with him about the number—later it was discovered that three of the victims were Italian subjects, two were U.S. citizens, and six were in the ambiguous category of having formally declared their intent to become American citizens. The Ambassador replied by restating the two demands of his government, whereupon Blaine exploded. "Impossible!" he shouted. "It is absolutely impossible for the federal government to interfere in the administration of justice in the individual states. I wonder that, after ten years of living in this country, you have not succeeded in making your government understand the impossibility!" The Ambassador stuck out his chin —the Italian gesture of one who has been offended. "I have nothing to reproach myself with on this question," he said flatly, "and you know it."

In an impatient manner, Blaine once again repeated his position. Fava answered calmly that this was no ordinary lynching because the victims were in the hands of government officials at the time. It would be pointless now to expect these same officials to punish themselves. Therefore, he said in an apparent reference to past federal actions, it was up to the President to intervene because "there is no law nor authority in New Orleans."

Fava had a point, and it irked Blaine. The federal government had intervened a number of times in the South since the Civil War, the last time in New Orleans being in 1875. In that year, General Philip H. Sheridan sent a famous telegram to Washington reporting that the U. S. Army took control of the city because "defiance to the laws and the murder of individuals seem to be looked upon by the community here from a standpoint which gives impunity to all who choose to indulge in either, and the civil government appears powerless to punish, or even arrest."

Blaine answered lamely, "But you ask of me a thing that is impossible, well knowing that I cannot change the Constitution." Seeing that the Secretary of State had apparently missed the point, Fava quickly corrected him, saying, "I do not ask you as much as that," but only that the American Government "find some means to have the guilty parties brought to trial."

Blaine answered sharply, "No, no, the federal government cannot do that! That is my answer!" It was now Fava's turn to lose patience. Of what use, then, he asked rhetorically, were the treaties between the United States and Italy? Blaine burst back, "That is your concern!" Fava stared at him for a minute or so, then decided his attempts at negotiation were useless. He dropped his bombshell—the ultimatum—"because your explicit words have compelled me to do so." Italy, he told Blaine, was recalling its Ambassador from Washington in protest—an action that was just short of a complete break of diplomatic relations. Blaine glared at him for a moment, then said in an angry voice, "All right, and we will recall our legation from Rome."

News of the Italian ultimatum was in the streets of Washington within minutes, each side being eager to tell its side of the issue to reporters. Upon hearing it, Senator Plumb of Kansas made a comment, printed in *The Nation,* which was widely applauded throughout the country: "His [Fava's] departure is of no more consequence to the American people than if the banana vendor who presides over a pushcart at 15th and F Streets should close out business and decide to go home."

Both countries lived up to the confrontation and recalled their ambassadors. Diplomatic relations between the two governments remained frozen at this impasse for over a year.

Meanwhile, President Harrison had to cope with a firestorm of conflicting emotions in his own country every bit as wild as the one Premier Rudini faced across the ocean.

15

In the days following March 14, scarcely a newspaper in the country failed to comment upon the New Orleans lynchings. A full 50 percent of the major American papers, in every section of the country, North, East, and West as well as South, approved the killing of the Italians. Among the approving papers were the New York *Times,* the Washington *Post,* the St. Louis *Globe-Democrat,* and the San Francisco *Chronicle.* The reasons given for approval were: the Italians' death made "life and property safer" in New Orleans (*Times,* March 18); the people of New Orleans had been "provoked" and had to break a "reign of terror" under which they lived (*Post,* March 17); the people of New Orleans were merely exercising their "rights" of "popular sovereignty and self-defense" (*Globe-Democrat,* March 15); and the eleven men were really guilty and were acquitted because they bribed the jury (*Times,* March 17; *Chronicle,* March 15). Even the London *Times,* in England, saw fit to express approval, which was reprinted proudly in the New Orleans *Times-Democrat* on March 19, 1891.

On the other side, most of the newspapers which denounced the lynchings did so only on the basis of general arguments against extra-legal mob action. Very few of them cited the anti-Italian motives of the mob leaders. The St. Louis *Republic* was one of the few exceptions. It wrote that the men were killed "on proof of being 'dagoes' and on the merest suspicion of being guilty of any other crime."

The leading organizations and institutions of the nation were more united than the newspapers in their endorsement of the lynchings, and in expressing hatred, contempt, and ridicule of Italian-Americans. The country was filled with ugly comment. On

April Fool's Day, the New York *Times* reported, in an article which it labeled "Fun with Italians," that both the National Maritime and Produce Exchanges in New York passed a resolution "declaring war" on Italy, the former because an Italian immigrant had erected a "neatly painted booth" next door, "from which it is supposed that he intends to maintain a trade in peanuts, fruit, etc." At the Consolidated Exchange, the brokers "made merry" with two Italian-Americans who happened to be on the premises. Elsewhere in the city, someone hired a poor, unemployed Italian immigrant to carry a sealed sack several blocks to City Hall. It contained 150 pounds of bricks. When the exhausted man arrived at the destination, he was greeted by a circle of laughing politicians and staff people.

Another Italian, it was reported, applied to a judge for citizenship papers in New York, and was turned away with a laugh when he couldn't answer the judge's mocking question "whether the United States was ruled by a king or a queen."

John R. Fellows, former district attorney of New York City, let it be known that he endorsed the mob action in New Orleans. Approval of the mass lynching was crowned by Theodore Roosevelt, one of the only two leading Republicans who continued to support Blaine in 1884 after the Mugwump reformers deserted him in disgust. Roosevelt called the lynching "a rather good thing" and boasted that he said so at a party in the presence of "various dago diplomats."

The grand jury investigating the lynchings began its work on March 17, as promised. From the beginning, it was clear that its role was to justify the lynchings rather than truly investigate them or indict those responsible for them. Its hearings were closed to the public, and all witnesses before it had to take an oath not to discuss their testimony with anyone. One of the early witnesses, Italian Consul Corte, respected the oath. But this did not prevent the judge presiding over the jury from commenting on his testimony. Corte had demanded that the lynchers be brought to justice. That same day Judge Robert H. Marr told news reporters that the lynchers would never be indicted. Quoting an eighteenth-century scholar's opinion that "there is no law under which a whole country can be indicted," the judge said it would be "impossible to prosecute five thousand persons." The judge maintained the fiction that thousands of people were equally responsible for the lynchings, despite the open role played by the sixty-one men who signed the call for the mob to gather, and the open role played by Parkerson, Wickliffe, Houston, and Denegre in leading the assault on the prison.

It was Judge Marr who had presided at the second trial of the Provenzanos (four months after Hennessy's murder), in which the defendants' unsupported claims that the Mantranga group constituted "the Mafia" led to the overturning of the previous conviction against the Provenzanos for shooting the Mantranga party.

As to the members of the prearranged "execution squad" who entered the prison and actually shot the Italians, the behavior of the officials of New Orleans is interesting. They daily made unproven assertions of conspiracies on the part of "oath-bound" secret Italian "vendetta societies." Thus they covered up precisely such a conspiracy on their own part. Additional confirmation of their conspiracy came many years later—in 1955. That year, an eighty-seven-year-old man died in Tampa, Florida, leaving a letter to be opened after his death. In it he wrote that he had been a member of an "execution squad" secretly selected on the night before the lynchings to enter the prison under cover of mob action to kill the Italians. The selection, he said, was made by members of the Committee of Fifty. He and the other selected "executioners" were sworn to an oath never to reveal the names of members of the squad, and were told an "Italian secret society" would kill them if their identities ever became known. The threat was effective—none of the "executioners" spoke about the premeditated behavior of Parkerson and the others on the night before the murder of the eleven Italians.

In case anyone still hoped that there would be justice in New Orleans, Judge Marr went on to say, "even if the Grand Jury were to indict the leaders of the lynchers, no jury could ever be secured to try them. Such publicity has been given to the affair that every one is conversant with the facts of the case, and no one is without a fixed opinion." A few months later, the same Judge Marr wrote, and the prestigious *American Law Review* printed, a long article in which he justified the lynchings. Professing his "sole purpose" in the article was "to present a perfectly true and impartial history of the Mafia case," he said of the lynch leaders:

There is absolutely no room to doubt the sincerity and the rectitude of purpose of those who enacted the tragedy. Among the leaders there was present not one member of the rough element. It was a movement conceived by gentlemen, and carried out by gentlemen— men who were led by what they conceived a solemn and terrible duty, and who were willing, in furtherance of what they thought public safety demanded, to undertake the performance of a most painful and revolting task. Every exchange and commercial body in New Orleans, on March 14th, endorsed what had been done that morning. Many of the signers of the call are among my own personal friends; with some of them I am connected by the ties of a long and intimate friendship; and thus I know the purity of their intentions, and must believe that the public danger which they sought to avert was a grim reality.

Neither the judge nor the editors of the law review identified his role in the case for the article's readers.

The grand jury issued indictments against six men—not murderers of the Italians, but six men who had worked for their defense attorneys. One was Dominick O'Malley, who returned to New Orleans and surrendered to the authorities to face the charges. The others were four associates of O'Malley in his private detective agency, including Thomas McCrystol and John Cooney, and one of the attorneys who helped defend the Italians at their trial, Bernard Claudi. The charges against the six were "attempted bribery" and other acts of jury tampering. The nation's newspapers headlined these charges, which were essentially repetitions of allegations made a few minutes after the trial by the district attorney that "one hundred thousand dollars" had been used to bribe the jury. This charge had been printed that same day in some New Orleans papers, including the *New Delta,* whose editor, Committee of Fifty member John C. Wickliffe, was to lead the lynchers in their violence the next morning. Now, however, the official charge was *attempted* bribery of *prospective* jurors, who in fact had not served on the trial jury, a comedown from the accusation that the jury was, in fact, bribed.

O'Malley was never tried. Two others were tried and acquitted, while McCrystol, Cooney and Claudi were convicted and sentenced to one year's hard labor.

Active in politics, Dominick O'Malley had for a long time been involved in political moves to have himself appointed Chief of Police. In this struggle, his foremost political enemies were Mayor Shakspeare and Chief Hennessy. The statement to the lynch mob that "O'Malley will be dealt with" made by Shakspeare's henchman, William S. Parkerson, supports speculation that the charges against him were Shakspeare's way of dealing with him. (If it was, it was repeated in 1904, when another Mayor had O'Malley, by that time a newspaper publisher, arrested to break the influence which he had gained over the New Orleans Police Department.) O'Malley had aggravated his enemies' hatred of him before the trial of the Italians by openly defying an "order" given to him in a threatening letter from the Committee of Fifty that he stop working for the defense lawyers. In October 1890, the Committee had written to him:

Sir:

The Committee of Fifty demand that you drop all connection instantly with the Italian vendetta cases, either personally or through your employees. They further demand that you keep away from the Parish Prison, the Criminal District Court and the Recorder's Court while these cases are on trial or under investigation; that you cease all communication with members of the Italian colony; that you cease, either in person or through your employees, to follow, interview or communicate with witnesses in the matter of the assassination of D. C. Hennessy. The Committee does not deny those accused the right to employ proper agencies, but they do not intend to allow a man of your known criminal record and unscrupulous methods to be an instrument for harm to the public at their hands.

O'Malley did indeed have a criminal record. He had been convicted five times for carrying concealed pistols, and twice for assault. Also, he had been twice indicted for jury tampering, but these charges were dropped by the then district attorney of the city, Lionel Adams, now O'Malley's partner and one of the principal defense lawyers in the Italians' trial. The only possible redeeming circumstances in this New Orleans' record was that O'Malley's "victims" and opponents were as criminal as he in the city's political and other corruption, and that carrying a pistol was a common practice, if technically illegal, in New Orleans.

Another fact held against the ruthless private detective was that he had been employed by the Mantrangas after they had been ambushed by the Provenzanos in May 1890. O'Malley claimed to have found the evidence that resulted in the Provenzanos' conviction at their first trial, a plausible claim in light of the police department's pro-Provenzano behavior at their trial.

Still more irritating, it was O'Malley's investigative work that had again and again foiled the persecution of the Italians by the Committee of Fifty. O'Malley had found major faults in the state's evidence. He collected evidence supporting the defendants' plea of innocence, and almost blew the cover of the Italian Pinkerton agent spying on the defendants in prison, whom O'Malley had begun to investigate just before the man had to be removed from his work because of the dysentery he contracted from prison food.

The private detective answered the Committee of Fifty with a defiant letter to the Committee's chairman:

In response I can but say that I propose to conduct the business of my office without instruction from you or the committee you pretend to represent.

Being unable to discover whence you derive any authority to

101

"demand" that I should obey your behests, with respect to the character of my employment, I shall continue to reserve to myself the right to think and act without regard to your wishes.

Later I shall have occasion to "demand" at your hands the evidence upon which you have ventured to write of my "known criminal record and unscrupulous methods."

Lionel Adams argued that there was no legal basis for prohibiting the accused Italians from hiring O'Malley. He also suggested that the district attorney alone was legally empowered to prosecute criminal cases, and not the Committee of Fifty.

O'Malley's defiance had been aggressive in that he had also, before the trial, filed a $10,000 suit for libel against the two editors of the *Daily States,* which was printing the Committee of Fifty's charges against him as if they were proven facts. Since one of these editors, George W. Dupre, was a member of the Committee of Fifty, O'Malley's suit in effect was a challenge to the Committee's practice of mongering rumors and lies. Even worse, O'Malley had made statements all along that Chief Hennessy's murder "is no Mafia or dago business," which must have chilled the hearts of the murderers if in fact they were not Italians.

As the grand jury continued its secret meetings for almost three months, those who controlled New Orleans closed ranks behind the lynchers. Judge Marr's statement later that "every commercial body" in the city endorsed the lynchings is indeed true. They included the four organizations which controlled most of the city's economy—the Cotton, Stock, and Lumbermen's Exchanges and the Board of Trade. The leader of the chorus was the Mayor, who daily praised the justice and virtue of the lynching.

A popular newspaper cartoon of the period shows a hefty woman labeled "Mafia" stalking the courtroom, terrorizing the jury in the Hennessy trial. She is wearing a black mask around her eyes, is dressed in eighteenth-century pirate garb, and carries a two-foot bloody sword in one hand and a pistol in the other.

Part of the great whitewash campaign involved persecuting the jurors who acquitted six of the nine Italians tried and couldn't reach a verdict regarding the remaining three. These men were called before the grand jury. Each swore that he had not been bribed, or influenced by anything but the testimony at the trial. Even more embarrassing to the whitewashers, seven of the ex-jurors repeated their claims of a fair decision in long interviews with newspaper reporters—the remaining five jurors remaining silent as they had been ordered by the grand jury.

The ex-foreman of the jury, a jeweler named Jacob M. Seligman, gave a long list of faults in the prosecution's case which made him vote for a verdict of innocence. They included the district attorney's failure to call William J. O'Connor, on whose word "Hennessy's accusation" against "dagoes" rested, or Officer Roe, who was alleged to have been wounded at the murder scene—by whom?

Seligman and other former jurors were punished for their statements. The jeweler found that his business partner had dissolved the partnership, that no one would do business with him any longer, and that he was the target of numerous threats of violence. He finally left the city, never to return. Another of the former jurors, a long-time Union Pacific Railroad clerk named Walter D. Livaudais, showed up for work the day after the verdict to be told that he was fired. Still another of the former jurors, Edward J. Donegan, reported repeated threats to his life to the police, who refused to furnish him with protection. Donegan finally hired armed private guards to patrol around his house.

While the grand jury's work and the problems with the Italian Government preoccupied news reporters, the New Orleans City Council quietly passed an ordinance (number 5256) on April 25, 1891, that speaks eloquently for the conclusion that the Italians were persecuted and lynched for economic motives, or at the very least, that the lynchers used their "public-spirited" deed to enrich themselves at the expense of the city's Italian community. The ordinance gave control of *all* of the multimillion-dollar business on the docks of New Orleans to the just-formed Louisiana Construction and Improvement Corporation. The ordinance was an attempt to freeze out Italian businessmen who, as Mayor Shakspeare and others had long complained, were gaining too much control of the lucrative waterfront commerce—the leading example being Joseph Macheca, lynched just one month before. As historian John S. Kendall was to note, "the ordinance by which the Louisiana Construction and Improvement Company acquired control of the wharves was full and elaborate." There were eight principal owners of this company. One of them, the president of the corporation, was James D. Houston, leader of the lynch mob and of the execution squad which actually killed the Italians, and whose political career included his shooting of several rivals to death. Houston's power was so cemented by the city's gift that within a year he was one of four men credited by historian George M. Reynolds with controlling all political power in the city for the next several years. Houston's crony in this rise to power was the late Chief Hennessy's secretary, George W. Vandervoort, source of the unsupported story that Hennessy was killed by the Mafia, which was "out to get him" ever since he spurned the "$50,000 bribe" of "Mafia leader" Giuseppe Esposito and brought him to justice nine years before he was killed.

Another of the eight owners of the new company was E. T. Leche, signer of the ad calling together the lynch mob. A third member of the eight who received the fabulous windfall from the city was Maurice J. Hart, a member of the Committee of Fifty and the man whose questionable testimony at the Devereaux murder trial in 1881 very likely saved David C. Hennessy from being convicted of first-degree murder.

One week after the City Council tried to throw Italian-American businessmen out of the port business of the city, and made fabulously wealthy men of some of the persecutors and murderers of the eleven Italians, the New Orleans Longshoremen's and Screwmen's Association, a labor union made up of white and black men, but no Italians, demanded that in the future *all* work of loading and unloading ships in New Orleans be given to them, and none of it given to Italian longshoremen, who the New York *Times* reported on May 3, 1891, enjoy "a monopoly of the trade, and they do not feel inclined either to join the Association [which in fact had barred them from joining as a matter of long-term practice] or to surrender what they have come to look upon as a sort of national right." The *Times* went on to report the Association's threat of violence: "The longshoremen, black and white, have already laid their plans, and declare that they will at an early day—perhaps on Monday—make a formal demand for the work, and if they are refused trouble will begin and blood will flow."

When the Italian community in New Orleans protested the attempted expulsion of their businessmen and workers from the port trade, they were treated to more threats and insults by Mayor Shakspeare. On May 16, His Honor called to his office the Provenzanos, and also respected Italian leaders, and reporters, to make a statement, which was reported in major newspapers throughout the United States. (The full text of this statement is in Appendix L). "I and every other decent citizen," he began, "am disgusted with the Dago disturbances and determined that they shall end immediately." He went on talking to Provenzano in terms which seemed to threaten all Italian-Americans:

> You are now using the longshoremen [issue] as a means of recapturing the fruit landing [trade]. You have shown your hands and I call you down. The longshoremen [the Association] have nothing to do with this business. They are not trying to cause trouble. . . . You have not learned the lesson taught your race by the people of New-Orleans, it seems, and I want you when you leave here to go home and tell your friends that if you make any more trouble, the police and Mayor of this city will not consider themselves responsible for the lives of you and yours. . . . I am not afraid to talk to you like this, because I am not afraid of you or the Italians. . . . I intend to put an end to these infernal dago disturbances, even if it proves necessary to wipe every one of you from the face of the earth.

That same month, the steamship *Plata* from Palermo, carrying 350 Sicilian immigrants, docked in New Orleans, bringing the total number of Sicilians who immigrated to the city in the seven months since Hennessy's murder to about three thousand. As was true of all their predecessors in those months, these bewildered and fearful immigrants were met by bullies sent by City Hall who pushed them around, searched them, insulted and threatened them —a policy that Shakspeare had inaugurated nine days after Hennessy's assassination when the ship *Elysian* arrived from Palermo with a thousand Sicilians.

Meanwhile, Shakspeare's henchman, lynch leader William Parkerson, went on a speaking tour of the country in which he stressed the need to restrict immigration, the responsibilities of civic duty, and the Americanism of the South. He told a gathering in Illinois on July 4, 1891:

I am neither a colonel or a judge, but a plain mister, a private citizen in the service of that great majesty, the people of the United States.

I yield in love of my country to no man within the borders of it. My pride in this grand government is not overlapped by any . . . and I hesitate not to assert that the most intensely American spirit and pride I have ever seen can be found in the lowlands of Louisiana. . . . The stars and stripes have no more faithful lovers than the men in the South. . . .

16

The grand jury finally issued its report on May 6, 1891. It is one of the most glaring examples of official mendacity in American history. (The full report is reprinted in Appendix M.) Without presenting at any time a single bit of credible evidence to support any of its many assertions, the grand jury repeated the charge that O'Malley had "fixed" the Italians' trial jury. It explained its failure to prove this by doublethink—"We must take occasion to say that it was not expected to obtain any evidence of undue influence from the members of the jury, for those who were uncorrupted had nothing to reveal, while the others would not make themselves particeps criminis . . ." The report said that in light of "the strong presentation of the case as made by the State" at the Italians' trial, "we cannot be mistaken in the assertion that the verdict was startling, amazing, a bitter disappointment, shocking to public opinion . . ." Next, the lie was repeated that "there is recorded in the office of the Italian Consul in this city the names of some 1,100 Italians and Sicilians landed here" with criminal records, and accused that "the Italian Government would rather be rid of them than be charged with their custody and punishment." It is alleged that "it cannot be questioned that secret organizations whose teachings are hostile to the fundamental principles of the Government of the United States must be a continual menace to the good order of society and the material welfare of the people. Whether the name be Mafia, Socialist, Nationalist, or whatever it may be . . ."

Hennessy, the report said, was killed because "his death was deemed necessary to prevent the exposure and punishment of criminals whose guilt was being fast established by his diligent pursuit." Noting that "the fruit and oyster business has drifted into the hands of the Italians, the volume of which in wholesale and retail lines reaches immense proportions," the report ignored the fact that the city was at that very moment forcibly trying to take these businesses away from the Italians, and asked, "What more do they want!"

After calling for restrictions of immigration to the United States, the grand jury claimed that "the gathering [of the lynch mob] on Saturday morning, March 14, embraced several thousands of the first, best and even the most law-abiding, of the citizens of this city, assembled, as is the right of American citizens, to discuss in public meeting questions of grave import." Ignoring the conspiracy of the mob leaders in planning the lynching of the prisoners and calling the mob together to cover their actions, the report said the decision to lynch was "general and spontaneous in character as truly indicating an uprising of the masses." The grand jury's conclusion flowed from these lies:

> The magnitude of this affair makes it a difficult task to fix the guilt upon any number of the participants—in fact, the act seemed to involve the entire people of the parish and city of New-Orleans, so profuse is their sympathy and extended their connection with the affair.
>
> In view of these considerations the thorough examination of the subject has failed to disclose the necessary facts to justify this Grand Jury in presenting indictments.

"The Lynchers Justified!" ran headlines all over the country. Some influential American newspapers echoed the New York *Post* in labeling the grand jury's report "the apology of a political committee for the act of revolutionary violence." Others, e.g., the Washington *Post,* endorsed it.

Italian-Americans everywhere became enraged at the report. Their many communities had been boiling since the lynchings. A delegation of twelve Italian-American leaders had accompanied Consul Corte to Washington in the week after the lynchings to

David C. Hennessy, Superintendent of the New Orleans Police Department. *Scribner's*, February 1896.

Joseph A. Shakspeare, Mayor of New Orleans. From *New Orleans: A Pictorial History*, by Leonard V. Huber (New York: Crown Publishers, 1971).

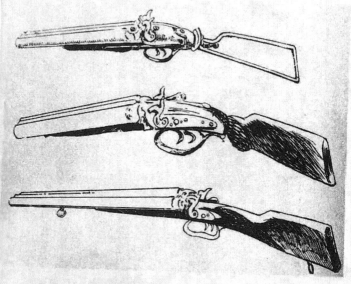

Three of the weapons used to kill David C. Hennessy. *Illustrated American*, November 8, 1890.

A certificate dated 1877, of doubtful authenticity, introducing one Gaetano Caffieri as a member of the Freemasons in Italy dedicated to "liberty or death." The Masons had been active in political revolutions since the American Revolution, and had used the skull-and-crossbones symbol since the French Revolution. *Illustrated American* printed the certificate on April 4, 1891, in a story about the Hennessy affair, with the fantastic caption: "Organized assassination: Certificate of the order of 'Decisi'—a provincial department of the Camorra—a general license to murder granted to the 'Registrar of the Dead.'" The Camorra was a notorious criminal group in Naples.

Hennessy stood on the sidewalk on the right, his assailants on the left sidewalk. *Illustrated American*, November 8, 1890.

The murderers fired at Hennessy from under or near the awning in front of Pietro Monasterio's shack. Two of the Chief's return shots hit the building on the right. *Illustrated American*, November 8, 1890.

The woman in this print is standing where Hennessy stood when shot. *Harper's Weekly*, March 28, 1891.

Chief Hennessy's home. A large number of unexplained bullets was found in the façade of this frame house, a half block from the murder scene. *Illustrated American*, November 8, 1890.

FOUR STREET SCENES IN THE ITALIAN SECTION OF NEW ORLEANS'
FRENCH QUARTER PRINTED IN THE "ILLUSTRATED AMERICAN" OF
APRIL 4, 1891, WITH CAPTIONS SLANTED TO AROUSE FEAR AND
HATRED OF ITALIAN-AMERICANS.

"Organized assassination: Scene in the Italian Quarter—Camorrists discussing the Hennessy murder."

"Travel through the Italian Quarter of any big city, and you may find yourself in the midst of a Camorra or Mafia."

"A Camorrist in the United States."

SKETCHES OF ORDINARY ITALIANS IN NEW ORLEANS PRINTED IN "ILLUSTRATED AMERICAN," WITH BIGOTED CAPTIONS, ON APRIL 4, 1891.

"Sharpening the stiletto of a New Orleans assassin."

"A Camorrist broomseller in the Italian Quarter."

TYPICAL SLUM DWELLINGS IN THE ITALIAN SECTION OF NEW ORLEANS SEEN IN PHOTOGRAPHS PRINTED BY "CHARITIES AND THE COMMONS" MAGAZINE OF NOVEMBER 4, 1905. THE CAPTIONS ARE THOSE OF THE JOURNAL.

"The court of an old French mansion in Little Palermo, showing how near to decay are the buildings which are filled to overflowing with Italian families."

"A court yard in Little Palermo, the Italian quarter of New Orleans. The greater part of this yard is covered with a clutter of oyster shells."

"The interior of a court showing passage out into the street. Women and children predominate in these houses because the men are many of them on the plantations."

FIVE OF THE ITALIAN-AMERICANS ACCUSED OF HENNESSY'S MURDER.

Antonio Scaffidi. *Illustrated American*,
April 4, 1891.

Pietro Monasterio. *Illustrated American*,
April 4, 1891.

Charles Mantranga. *Illustrated American*, April 4, 1891.

Joseph P. Macheca. *Harper's Weekly*, March 28, 1891.

Antonio Bagnetto. *Harper's Weekly*, March 28, 1891.

Thomas Duffy, the twenty-nine-year-old newsboy who shot Antonio
Scaffidi in Parish Prison after attending Hennessy's funeral on the
same day. *Harper's Weekly*, March 28, 1891.

Exterior view of Parish Prison. *Harper's Weekly*, March 28, 1891.

Interior view of Parish Prison. *Illustrated American*, April 4, 1891.

Gabriel Villere, Criminal Sheriff of New Orleans. *Illustrated American*, April 4, 1891.

Captain Lemuel Davis, warden of Parish Prison. *Illustrated American*, April 4, 1891.

A crowd, eventually to number twelve to twenty thousand, responding to a newspaper advertisement, gathers around the statue of Henry Clay on the morning of March 14, 1891. William S. Parkerson is seen urging an assault on Parish Prison. *Harper's Weekly*, March 28, 1891.

The lynch mob battering the Treme Street gate of Parish Prison. *Scribner's*, February 1896.

Ferreting doomed Italian prisoners out of their hiding places in Parish Prison. *Illustrated American*, April 4, 1891.

The killing of six of the Italians in the main yard of Parish Prison. *Harper's Weekly*, March 28, 1891.

The bodies of Joseph P. Macheca, Antonio Scaffidi, and Antonio Marchesi lying where they were shot in a gallery in Parish Prison. Macheca had picked up an Indian club in a futile effort to defend himself. *Illustrated American,* April 4, 1891.

Arranging the bodies of some of the slain Italian-Americans in Parish Prison for public viewing. *Illustrated American,* April 4, 1891.

THE THREE MEN WHO, TOGETHER WITH JAMES D. HOUSTON, COM-
MANDED THE "EXECUTION SQUAD" ON MARCH 14, 1891.

John C. Wickliffe. *Harper's Weekly,*
March 28, 1891.

William S. Parkerson. *Harper's Weekly,*
March 28, 1891.

Walter D. Denegre. *Illustrated American,*
April 4, 1891.

Benjamin Harrison, President of the United States.

James G. Blaine, U.S. Secretary of State. From *James G. Blaine*, by
Edward Stanwood. By permission of Houghton Mifflin Company.

Marchese Antonio di Starabba Rudini, Premier of Italy. *Illustrated American,* April 4, 1891.

Baron Francesco Fava, Italy's Ambassador to the United States. *Illustrated American,* April 4, 1891.

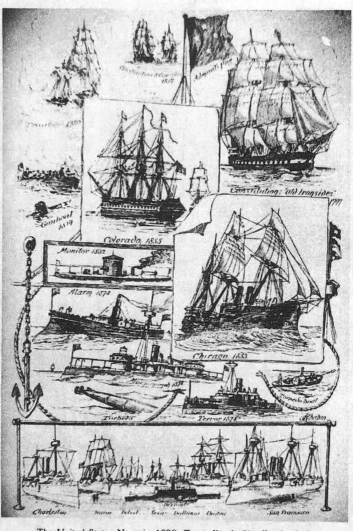

The United States Navy in 1890. From *King's Handbook of the United States* (Buffalo, N.Y.: Moses King Corporation, 1891).

press demands for justice upon President Harrison. Now, on the evening of the grand-jury report, Corte sent an open letter to the jury's chairman, and copies to the city's newspapers. Corte's indictment of the grand jury is telling. (The full letter is in Appendix N.) The Consul noted that some members of the grand jury had been in the mob that lynched the Italians. He also cited the open actions of those who planned the lynchings of the Italians and the work of the prearranged execution squad. "The names of the participants in the killing, as well as those of the instigators," he said, "are of public notoriety."

The letter made Mayor Shakspeare uneasy, and on May 16 he sent a private letter to Governor Nicholls, citing Corte's letter, and requesting that the Governor "ask of the Honorable Secretary of State at Washington, the recall of Consul Corte's Exequartor [accreditation] by the President." (The full letter is in Appendix O.) The Italian Government, apparently at the urging of Washington, on May 11 recalled Corte to Rome under the pretext of his reporting firsthand on the events in New Orleans.

The grand jury report did not mention a letter given them by Consul Corte, signed by "John Duffy," and received by Corte in November 1890. This may have been Thomas Duffy, the man who shot Scaffidi in Parish Prison. Newspaper stories sometimes unaccountably referred to Thomas Duffy as John Duffy. The letter charged that Dominick O'Malley was a principal in Hennessy's murder, and that Thomas McCrystol, Louis Lay, E. P. Wallace, and Thomas G. Washburne were the gunmen. Corte now made the letter public, and District Attorney Luzenberg admitted Corte showed it to him back in November 1890 but said that he investigated it at the time and found it groundless.

Left without the leading representatives of the Italian Government pleading their cause in the United States, Italian-Americans renewed the mass protest meetings which had been numerous in America's large cities after the lynchings. Speakers at these meetings in New York, Philadelphia, Pittsburgh, Boston, Chicago, Nashville, St. Louis, Detroit, Kansas City, St. Paul, San Francisco, and dozens of other cities called upon President Harrison to intervene to bring the lynchers to justice and give a financial indemnity to the victims' families.

The American press, sensationalistic and largely viciously anti-Italian-American, highlighted the more excessive speakers, sometimes even inventing when the actual speeches were not wild enough, or when the reporter didn't understand the Italian language. Although many papers failed to report that most of the Italian-American meetings opened with salutes to the American flag and other deliberate expressions of loyalty to the United States, all the papers headlined reports that a group of one thousand Italian laborers building a railway in Ohio had armed themselves and were drilling as a military unit. On April 4, 1891, the New Orleans *Times-Democrat* highlighted a baseless story it attributed to a reporter in Pittsburgh that 20,000 Italian-Americans from that city were planning an armed attack on New Orleans.

American newspapers also gave prominence to two or three cases of Americans abused in Italy, as when the New York *Times* printed a story, the day after the grand jury's report, of the stoning of a carriage in Florence carrying an American executive of the Bell Telephone Company and his family which injured the Boston man's young daughter.

Very often the papers accompanied the stories of protest meetings with editorial comment insulting and ridiculing Italian-Americans. For example, the Portland *Oregonian* called their protests "an explosion of cheap Latin fury and braggadocio, which will come to nothing," and warned them that they might provoke "a revival of mob violence . . . on a scale which will make the Mafia massacre look like play." The New York *Times* also warned Italian-Americans to stop their "strange" behavior before it provokes "a hostile feeling against Italians as Italians." Similarly, the Cincinnai *Times-Star* warned them that their behavior "could have one ending, and that is too terrible to contemplate." The Kansas City *Times* threatened that they would be reduced to "white faced fools begging protection"; the St. Paul *Pioneer-Press* said their protests were "in the infernal spirit of the Mafia"; while the St. Louis *Globe-Democrat* joined a chorus of other papers suggesting that the citizenship of the protesters be revoked and they be deported. The Washington *Star* mocked them: "Italy has a fruit standing army in the United States." The Washington *Post*'s ridicule ran to a dialogue in dialect between two fictional Italian-American organ grinders:

SIGNOR TUNITUPPI: We havea been insult.
SIGNOR GRINDOVERRA: Villa ve be revenge?
SIGNOR TUNITUPPI: Ve–a vill. Loada up de organ with more "Sweeta Violet" and "Whitea Winga."

This behavior of the American press encouraged "retaliation" against Italian-Americans, thousands of whom were abused, sometimes even beaten, in the streets of American cities. Unknown numbers of them were fired from their jobs or denied employment. On May 13, Pennsylvania authorities had to assign forty deputy sheriffs to protect two hundred Italian immigrants who were on their way from Pittsburgh to work in the H. C. Frick Company coal mines in Fayette County. In Wheeling, West Virginia, a mob attacked a group of Italian-American workers on May 11, killing three of them and injuring an unknown number. The police in Troy, New York, forcibly broke up a peaceful protest meeting of Italian-Americans. The cops fired upon the protesters, claiming they were "armed with knives and guns." At least one of the crowd was shot.

The vicious anti-Italian hysteria continued and was unabated in March 1892 when relatives of eight of the lynched Italians sued the city of New Orleans for a quarter of a million dollars in a *federal* district court. The plaintiffs, including Gaspare Marchesi, and Scaffidi's and Bagnetto's widows, claimed damages on the grounds that the Mayor and other city officials deliberately failed to protect their relatives from the lynch mob. In another suit, the widow of another of the victims, one who had not been tried, sued several leaders of the lynch mob in federal court, including Parkerson, Houston, and Denegre, for one hundred thousand dollars.

111

The federal courts rejected the claims in both suits, and refused to grant the petitioners a penny. All avenues to American justice had now been exhausted by Italian-Americans, except their appeal to President Harrison.

17

The New Orleans grand jury's condoning of the lynching was echoed by Governor Nicholls of Louisiana, who said from the beginning that he would be guided by its report—knowing in advance what it would be. Now he informed President Harrison that the state of Louisiana considered the incident closed. Yet the President could not let it rest there. Even if Harrison could turn a deaf ear to the protests of Italian-Americans and the Government of Italy, several things had developed that forced his hand. In fact, he was caught in a crisscross of forces destroying his political life.

The pressure upon the President would have been relieved considerably if it could be shown that the lynched Italians were really guilty of the Hennessy murder. They would, then, have "gotten what they deserved." Justice would have been done, in popular opinion, no matter how crudely or illegally. Accordingly, just after the lynching, Harrison ordered the U. S. Attorney General, William H. H. Miller, to investigate the possibility. The President could not have made a better choice in the interest of pursuing the truth. Although the fifty-one-year-old Miller had been a law partner of Harrison in Indianapolis, his years as Attorney General had gained for him a strong reputation for impartial fairness and refusal to bow to political influences, uncommon virtues in Harrison's administration.

Miller placed the local investigation in the hands of the Federal District Attorney for Louisiana, William Grant.

Upon hearing this news, Mayor Shakspeare launched a campaign to persuade the federal investigators that the Italians were guilty. On April 10, he wrote to District Attorney Grant, once again citing his "list of 94 cases of murder and attempted murder by this class of people in New Orleans." Grant and his assistants studied the list. They also studied the transcript of the Italians' trial, which had been recorded verbatim at the insistence of the defense lawyers, and all the "evidence" collected by the grand jury. Shakspeare also wrote to Grant that Pietro Monasterio, the cobbler who had lived next to the Hennessy murder site, had "over $50,000" on him when he was arrested. This charge had been made by the prosecutor during the trial, who claimed the money was taken from the Italian in a large purse. The defense counsel had torn the allegation apart by demanding that the money or the purse be produced—something which the authorities could not do during the trial or after it. Nor did they attempt to explain what had happened to the alleged evidence.

Despite Shakspeare's efforts, Grant gave a report of his findings which placed Harrison firmly on the spot. On April 27, just a few days before the grand jury's whitewash report, Grant reported privately to Washington. (The full text of his report is in Appendix P). He wrote of the evidence at the Italians' trial that "as a whole and in detail it is exceedingly unsatisfactory, and is not, to my mind, conclusive one way or the other." "As to the alleged bribery of the jury," he wrote, "which tried the persons accused of the murder of Hennessy, I have to report that my examination does not connect any of the persons killed with that charge, if true." In addition, he said he was "unable to obtain any direct evidence connecting these persons with the Mafia, or any other association of a similar character in the city." The only evidence that such an organization even existed in New Orleans, he went on, was the statements that it did made by the Provenzano brothers. They, however, had a vested interest in labeling Charles Mantranga as a chief of the Mafia. This allegation alone had won their acquittal at their second trial of the charge of ambushing the Mantranga group, a charge for which they had been previously found guilty and sentenced to life imprisonment.

Grant's report gave strong moral support to the demands of Italian-Americans and the government in Rome that President

Harrison intervene in Louisiana to bring the lynch leaders to justice. Yet he dare not intervene, for the political consequences of doing so would be disastrous for him.

President Benjamin Harrison, a corporate lawyer from Indiana, was a former brigadier general in the Union Army whose political career after the war capitalized upon the creditable war record of the "Hoosier Warrior." He had barely gotten to the White House in 1888 in a fluke election, collecting more electoral votes by political maneuvering than his opponent, Grover Cleveland. But Cleveland had actually gotten more popular votes and was the people's choice. In addition, Harrison had run the most corrupt campaign in American history before Watergate, and the consensus in the country was that he had both lost the election and stolen the White House. He lost especially badly in the South—in Louisiana by a ratio of almost three votes to one. In 1891, Cleveland was already laying the groundwork for a comeback in the election next year, and in fact was to beat Harrison in the contest.

Although Harrison resembled James G. Blaine in physical appearance, with the same white hair and full, inverted "V" beard, he did not enjoy Blaine's enormously popular following, and did not match his Secretary of State's brilliant intelligence. And his personality was poles apart from the magnetic, flamboyant Blaine. Harrison was cold and aloof. He was the grandson of the popular William H. "Tippecanoe" Harrison, the popular Indian fighter who had won election to the White House in a rip-roaring campaign in 1840, only to die after a month in office. At the beginning of grandson Benjamin's campaign for the presidency, his supporters tried to nickname him "Young Tippecanoe," but had to abandon the public relations gimmick because their candidate was so icy and austere. Worse, he was vain, haughty, and even arrogant. When he had received the news that he had in fact been elected, he startled friends who were present by muttering loudly to himself, "Now I walk with God." As President, he reportedly never offered a chair to any visitor to his White House office. He made one and all stand while he sat behind his desk. Although he was a famous legal hairsplitter, Harrison's administration was laced with corruption, and became infamous as the cat's-paw of wealthy special interests. By 1890, the new Populist Party was justly charging that from the "prolific womb of governmental injustice, we breed two great classes—tramps and millionaires."

Harrison was, in a word, inept. Blaine and a few other Republican powers ran the government at least as much as, if not more than, did the President.

Adding to Harrison's problems with the South was the fact that he headed the Republican Party at a time when it was "waving the bloody shirt" of guilt at the South for causing the Civil War. The festering wounds of the Reconstruction period of federal control of the South had only just begun to heal. Federal intervention in New Orleans would rip them wide open.

Compounding the President's dilemma was the fact that Blaine, his own Secretary of State, was openly challenging him for leadership of the Republican Party, part of Blaine's move toward the unsuccessful attempt he was to make the next year at the Republican convention to take the party's presidential nomination away from Harrison and capture it for himself.

Blaine's tactics were to criticize and sabotage Harrison's foreign policy and to aggravate Harrison's great unpopularity in the country. A notorious anti-Southerner and anti-Catholic, Blaine was a natural spoiler in the "Italian problem."

In 1888, Blaine had made a deal not to oppose Harrison for the presidential nomination, and as a reward was appointed Secretary of State by Harrison when he took office. Now, in 1891, everything that Blaine did hurt Harrison. His tough talk to Louisiana's officials caused the President to be hated even more in the South, and his tough talk to Italy inflamed the international problem and hardened American opinion against any reconciliation with Rome.

American attitudes toward the problem with Italy had become dangerously irrational and belligerent because of a "war scare" which was running wild in the nation. At the time, America was virtually unarmed, while Italy had one of the strongest military machines in the world. The Italian Army had 2,500,000 soldiers, contrasted with 128,000 in the U. S. Army. Of even more importance, the United States had virtually no fighting navy in 1889 —just three very small steel warships backed by obsolete, unarmed wooden support ships. The weight of the three warships *totaled* only 7,863 tons, and *all together* they carried four 8-inch and thirteen 6-inch guns, all foreign-made. These three tiny warships —really gunboats—were supported by, in the words of the official U. S. Navy report of 1892, "a few old ships long since obsolete and fast going to decay." There were only eight thousand men in the entire U. S. Navy. Although a naval building program was underway in the U.S., it was small and the navy was not much larger in 1891.

Italy, on the other hand, had twenty-two of the most modern warships in the world, including eleven huge battleships, *each* of which weighed 11,000 to 14,000 tons. These first-line ships were backed by fifty-four modern, fast support ships, all heavily armed. And the Italian Navy was building dozens more warships, having created the industry to manufacture total warships, unlike the United States, which in 1889 did not have a single factory capable of making a modern naval gun.

Shortly after the lynchings in New Orleans, American newspapers began to print reports that the large Italian fleet was making ready to attack the coastal cities of the United States. Some printed rumors that the ships were actually on their way across the Atlantic. These stories continued to make headlines for about a year, causing an epidemic of alarm, panic, and anger throughout the country. The popular magazine *Illustrated American* devoted an entire issue to the discussion of war with Italy, comparing in detail the American military weakness vis-à-vis the Italian Navy.

After noting, "In the spring the Dago fancy / Fiercely turns to thoughts of war," the Portland *Oregonian* was typical of many papers in the United States that promised that the Italian Navy would be destroyed.

The Italian Government issued repeated official denials that it was planning to make war on the United States, the first of which was given just six days after the lynchings. As the months passed, these denials included long statements of Italy's intent to achieve a peaceful reconciliation with America. President Harrison and the Secretaries of War, the Navy, and the Treasury all repeated long statements that American observers reported that Italy's fleet was still in European waters and was not making any of the elaborate preparations needed for a transatlantic war, and that the United States had absolutely no expectation of going to war with Italy. These assurances were mostly disregarded in America, partly because of Harrison's low "credibility" throughout the country. Egged on by the country's largely jingoistic press, and by statements of politicians like Senator Adolph Meyer, who later recalled that "within the space of a very few days war seemed inevitable," thousands of individuals and groups sent telegrams and letters pouring into the White House volunteering to fight in a war against Italy!

A telegram from Sparta, Georgia, offered to raise "a company of unterrified Georgia rebels to invade Rome, disperse the Mafia, and plant the Stars and Stripes on the dome of St. Peter's." Five hundred men volunteered from Jefferson County, Montana. Another telegram from that state declared that "for the love of the American Eagle, fifty Cow Boys offer their services. Let the Dagoes come!" The second regiment of the New York Irish Volunteers telegraphed its desire to fight, as did one thousand "able men" from Pocahontas, Virginia. A thousand men each volunteered from Laclede County, Missouri, and Caldwell, Kansas, while ten thousand were offered from elsewhere in Kansas. Huron, South Dakota, offered one hundred would-be soldiers.

Letters of volunteers even came from men in Ireland and England. Italians were hated in Ireland for "murdering the brave Chief Hennessy," recently elevated to a status of near sainthood by Irishmen on both sides of the Atlantic. And Italians were hated in England—where London's *St. James Gazette* wrote that "the Italian has murder in his blood and that [his] racial excitability is heightened by a warm climate." At the heart of the British hatred was Italy's new navy, perceived as a potential threat to England's maritime Empire.

Many newspapers and politicians joined in fanning the war frenzy when they realized that it was uniting Americans from the North and South for the first time since the Civil War. And many of the messages sent to Washington in fact supported the use of the war scare to reunite a nation divided by bitter hatred. Not only did Union veterans volunteer, as did one California amputee who offered his remaining arm to carry a rifle, but ex-Confederate soldiers were volunteering in astonishing numbers in an apparent desire to atone for their previous rebellion by, as one letter put it, "fighting for the old flag as willingly as I fought against it." A thousand Tennessee veterans volunteered as a group, as well as thousands of others from other former Confederate states.

Black former slaves also volunteered, as one in Virginia expressed it, "to serve in defense of the flag that made me free."

Although the press was silent about the possibility of ex-slaves entering the military, many influential papers editorially urged that President Harrison "give the old Confederate officers and privates a chance to meet the enemy," as the Charleston *News and Courier* put it. Papers in all parts of the country echoed Oregon's *Telegram-Register,* which declared that the "effects of a war with Italy would be good. . . . It would not be the 'Blue and the Gray' but a solid mass of 'Blue.' The national uniform would be worn and national tunes would march the loyal masses of the South to the front."

Harrison's efforts to dispel the war scare were compromised by his desire to cultivate its possibilities for increasing his popularity. The temptation to pose as a leader of a threatened nation was excited by "close ranks" telegrams like the one from Wisconsin's Cushing Naval Veterans Association which was addressed to "Comrade" Benjamin Harrison and said, "Stand by your guns. We are with you."

Harrison's statements to dissolve the war scare were, to his credit, direct and honest. But his anti-rumor efforts were almost sunk when the country learned that the Secretary of War ordered a strengthening of the country's harbor defenses—almost nonexistent except for a few crumbling Civil War forts.

Although it is impossible to know Washington's hand, if any, in creating the war scare, there is no doubt that it used the scare to do something the Harrison administration had been lobbying for since 1888: the construction of a large, new, modern navy. Harrison, Blaine, Secretary of War Redfield Proctor, and Secretary of the Navy Benjamin Franklin Tracy, together with a few key members of Congress, such as Congressman Henry Cabot Lodge of Massachusetts, second-ranking member of the House Naval Committee, were leaders of the navy lobby. Lodge's career had been advanced because of his loyalty to James G. Blaine in 1884. He, and Theodore Roosevelt, continued to support Blaine's presidential candidacy in the face of the proven corruption on his part which drove the reform wing of the Republican Party to defect. After Blaine became Secretary of State in 1888, Lodge's already great power was boosted by his associate's new position.

Lodge, incidentally, was one of the most vicious anti-Italians in Congress. His five years in the House and thirty-one years in the Senate were marked by insulting speeches and articles by him about Italian-Americans. Because most were of southern Italian background, Italian-Americans were considered inferior by Lodge, as distinct from the people of northern Italy, whom he termed "Teutonic Italians." Lodge had taken the occasion of the New Orleans lynchings to write an article in the very prestigious *North American Review* in which he used the incident as a platform to condemn the "new immigrants" from Southern and Eastern Europe, who he claimed were inferior to the older Northern European stock. Singling out Italians especially as "criminals and anarchists," he also warned his readers that unless something were done some four million Jews from Eastern Europe would eventually come to the United States, taking it for granted that the prediction would alarm Americans. He concluded by calling for laws to end the immigration of all these undesirables.

Despite their very aggressive efforts, the cause of the navy lobby had been mostly unsuccessful before the "Italian problem." Feeling that America had nothing to fear from powers across the oceans, and that its traditional policy of "passive" coastal defense was sufficient, Congress had seen little need for a navy, and repeatedly rejected naval construction bills introduced or backed by the lobby.

Now, however, the legislators were having second thoughts as the administration argued, as in Navy Secretary Tracy's speech to them, that the United States needed a modern *long-range offensive* fleet "to beat off the enemy's fleet on its approach . . . by threatening his own coast, for a war, though defensive in principle, may be conducted most effectively by being offensive in its operations." This policy was in clear contradiction to long-standing American policy of "defensive defense" only. The Harrison administration now demanded that Congress approve building a new navy of twenty battleships and sixty fast cruisers, all long-range ships.

Key newspapers supported the campaign of the navy lobby, some for jingoistic motives, others from panic, still others from hatred of Italians. Some did so to unite the divided country and heal the Civil War wounds; some because of associations with shipbuilders and others standing to make huge profits from a new navy. Even more moderate newspapers used the war scare for purposes of arming the country, as when the New York *World,* which made clear it did not believe there would be a war, wrote:

If there were a real cause for war, in what condition would a declaration of hostilities find us? Italy is not a first-rate power, but she has one of the strongest fleets in Europe, against which our ports and coasts are very inadequately prepared for defense. It is humiliating beyond endurance that our great country, in some respects the strongest power in the world, should be thus crippled for want of an adequate means of defense against a second-rate European power.

Congressman Lodge, dividing his efforts between anti-immigration and pro-navy activity, jumped to support Tracy's proposal with his characteristic mendacity. In the words of naval historians Harold and Margaret Sprout, Lodge in a speech to Congress, "posing as an authority on naval affairs, asserted with palpable inaccuracy that the battleship proposal introduced nothing new, but

121

was 'merely the continuance' of a policy 'settled' by the War of 1812, and followed consistently thereafter."

For the first time, the limping efforts of the navy lobby gained real momentum through the popular scare of war with Italy, and the drive proved to be unstoppable. The effects on history were momentous, marking one of the greatest turning points in both American and world affairs. The famous "New Navy of the 1890s" was rapidly built, and just seven years later it smashed the enemy fleet in the Spanish-American War of 1898, a war strongly called for and supported by Senator Henry Cabot Lodge and the man who had been chairman of the Republican Party and Secretary of War under Harrison, Redfield Proctor. Proctor was also instrumental in getting the United States to intervene in Cuba in 1898. The New Navy, advanced by the sordid events in New Orleans, thus gained the Philippines, Puerto Rico, and control over Cuba for the United States. The country was launched upon an irreversible path as a power with a worldwide empire and interests. Gone forever was the American policy of isolationism held since the days of George Washington. America's fantastic career as a global power, the "American era" in world history, dawned with the scare of war with Italy, exploited, if not created, by the navy lobby in the White House and Congress.

Another lesson of the war scare found at least one astute student in the person of Theodore Roosevelt. In 1895, as he looked at the divisive American problems of corruption, the economy, and labor struggles, he commented, "What this country needs is a war."

18

As months passed following the lynchings in New Orleans, Premier Rudini was confronted with domestic political problems in Rome as bad as Harrison's in Washington. His political enemies in the Italian Parliament were calling for his resignation, blaming his administration for the country's severe economic problems. Italy was heavily in debt, mostly because of the long, expensive arms race with France and the Austro-Hungarian Empire—which had produced the Italian Navy now frightening so many Americans. Years of mismanagement of Italy's economy had also resulted in disastrous unemployment, especially in the nation's south, from whose population many were emigrating to American cities like New Orleans. One way out of Italy's economic mess, as Rudini saw it, lay in increased foreign trade. And the greatest hope lay in trade with the new colossus in the making across the sea, the incredibly booming United States.

On March 1, 1891, when the trial in New Orleans had only just begun, newspapers in Italy and the United States reported on the success of the Italian Government's carefully executed campaign to increase trade with the United States. The opening sentences of the New York *Times* version of the story are revealing. "All the American Counsuls in Italy," wrote the paper, "have joined in a report to the [U.S.] Government on the conditions of trade between Italy and the United States, with the view of calling the attention of American merchants to the opening afforded here for an extension of that foreign commerce. The Consuls, both in the northern and southern portions of Italy, are confident that the subject has been presented in such a manner that it cannot fail to command public attention." Two weeks later, the good citizens of New

Orleans were to lynch the eleven Sicilian-Americans, leading to the diplomatic clash between the United States and Italy. Rudini's plans to fortify the Italian economy with American trade were stopped.

Moreover, the New Orleans affair actually directly pushed Italy into economic crisis. As early as April 6, before the recalled Ambassador had left for Rome, a prominent Italian editor in Paris, with close ties to his government, told reporters that "in Italy widespread commercial troubles, long chronic, are becoming critical, and that apart from Italy's overwhelming public debt, which would disable her in an attempt to go to war [with the U.S.] unless backed by other European powers, any measure imperiling peace would produce a general economic crash. Already an effect of the American-Italian difficulty is felt in the hesitation of French financial houses to proceed with the negotiations pending for the prospective Italian loan, in which German houses are already concerned."

By September, the stresses on the Italian economy and government were unbearable for Premier Rudini, and on the seventh of that month he sent a secret message to President Harrison, through an American intermediary in Rome, confiding that Italy would accept a face-saving solution to the impasse with America. Very significantly, in this message, Rudini dropped the demand that the leaders of the New Orleans lynch mob be brought to justice. All that remained of the dispute between the two nations was the demand for financial indemnity to the victims' families. This conciliatory, almost pleading position was the secret reality behind the Italian Government's tough public statements.

Harrison's answer, on the other hand, given as an instruction to Blaine, was hard. He demanded that Italy send its Ambassador back to Washington "as the first step towards any friendly discussion." "I think," he added to his Secretary of State, "we should carefully avoid any implication that our action could be favorable upon the renewed suggestion of indemnity." Italy, undeterred, continued to make secret overtures for reconciliation. Harrison, with seeming churlishness, or perhaps because of the unifying effect the crisis was having on Americans, its use to the navy lobby, and the increase of public support it brought him, decided to play it cool and let the crisis develop further rather than resolve it early, as could easily have been done. On October 14, he wrote to Blaine, "They [the Italian Government] acted hastily and foolishly and ought not to have too much help in a necessary retreat."

Thus, as a deliberate policy, Harrison allowed the crisis to fester over the next months. Finally, he made his first conciliatory statement in his annual message to a joint session of Congress on December 9, 1891. In those times, the annual message was not delivered by the President himself but read to Congress by an assistant sent by him. The press reported that many of the senators and congressmen present ignored the reading of Harrison's message—some slept, others carried on loud conversations with each other—until the speaker began reading a surprise section of the speech dealing with the New Orleans affair. These two paragraphs caught most of the listeners' attention. "The lynching at New Orleans," the President began, "in March last of eleven men of Italian nativity [*sic:* Macheca was American-born] by a mob of citizens was a most deplorable and discreditable incident." He went on to label the lynching an "offense against law and humanity." Although the President reverted to his customary legalism in the rest of the speech, discussing treaties and making a recommendation to Congress that it enact laws giving the federal courts jurisdiction in crimes committed against foreigners on American soil, his strong denunciation of the killings was unequivocal and made headlines on both sides of the Atlantic.

Rudini's "decidedly favorable" response to Harrison's speech was quietly, but quickly, conveyed to the White House. Italian-Americans, not knowing that Italy had in fact dropped its demand for the lynchers' punishment, were encouraged by Harrison's speech. Also unknown to them, the President had even, in fact, decided not only that an indemnity was to be paid to the victims' families, but also the amount of the grant. Noting that the United States accepted a cash indemnity from Spain for the lives of some American sailors lost at Spanish hands—"we took $2500 a piece for the sailors, thus setting a price"—he proposed in a letter to Blaine "the same for the Italians killed at New Orleans." Everything seemed ready for a reconciliation between the two nations, except the extremely hostile response to Harrison's speech on the part of many Americans—including congressmen and newspaper editors.

Harrison's relations with Congress were extremely poor, and Congress' reaction to his overture is partly the result of its desire to embarrass him in the continuing struggle between it and him for pre-eminence. The President was accused of "giving in" to the "blustering" of Italy and Italian-Americans. Blaine had put Harrison in a corner in the previous months by saying repeatedly that the President would take no action without the approval of Congress. And since the anti-Harrison, anti-Italian, jingoistic, and navy lobby factions constituted a majority of Congress, approval was out of the question. In the face of vocal disapproval of his speech, Harrison once again decided to let time pass.

Six months later, and thirteen months after the lynching, the President finally acted, and again he did so without consulting Congress. On April 13, 1892, he made a move that startled the country. He announced that "without committing itself to the recognition of any claim for indemnity, but simply as an act of justice, and from motives of comity," he had turned over to a representative of the Italian Government a cash indemnity to be distributed among the Italian victims' families of slightly less than $25,000—just under the $2,500 per family, which was the figure he had secretly decided upon months before. Knowing that Congress would never appropriate money for this purpose, Harrison had taken the money from a $80,000 special fund given the White House by Congress each year for "unforeseen emergencies."

Congress was furious. It acted quickly to stop the President. Seventeen days after Harrison's announcement, the House of Representatives passed a resolution reducing the President's emergency fund to $60,000, and debated a proposal that no part of this money should be paid "in settlement of any claim of such a foreign power against the United States." Harrison was accused of "unconstitutional executive usurpation of Congressional powers" and of acting falsely when there was no "real emergency." There was even talk of impeaching him. But, although the President was only weakly defended in Congress, he had acted so abruptly as to present Congress with a *fait accompli*. There simply wasn't much more Congress could do, and its censure of the President fizzled out.

Much of the press and population took a path similar to that of Congress. They were angry at first, then resigned, though disapproving.

The Italian Government quickly made known its pleasure at Harrison's act, and did not mention again its demand that the lynchers be brought to justice. Former Ambassador Fava in Rome was quoted by the New York *Times* as saying that his government was "jubilant over the settlement, and is satisfied that the old-time good feeling between the two Governments has been fully restored." This was the same man who, two days after the lynching, had advised Italian-Americans not "to be carried away by the first impulses of outraged feelings . . . but wait in a calm and dignified manner for justice to be done." He had ended his plea to them with "an appeal to you to have unlimited faith in the [Italian] Government of the King." A quick reconciliation took place between the two governments, and within five days each renamed its Ambassador to the other's capital.

Italian-Americans felt betrayed and were outraged at both governments. They angrily denounced the agreement in public meetings as a "sell-out" by Rome to bolster the Italian economy, and a "buy-off" by Harrison countenancing mass murder. At first the American press ridiculed these statements, one paper calling them "chin music," and warned the dissenters against "causing further trouble." Then the newspapers turned their backs on the protests and ignored them altogether, as did both the American and Italian governments. Italian-Americans, thousands of whom had begun their petitions to President Harrison with the phrase "We, Italians by birth, Americans by choice," became convinced that neither

127

designation protected their basic human rights. There was a galling reaffirmation among them of a belief, born of centuries of southern Italian experience, which they had hoped would have been canceled when they came to the new land which promised "equal justice for all." "The law," generations of *contadini* had repeated, "works against the people."

19

Aftermath

The political and economic repression of Louisiana's Italian-Americans was severe, and the group's comeback was slow. Fourteen years after the lynching a study reported in *Charities and the Commons* described typical economic and living conditions of Italians on a single block in the French Quarter:

Going to the court yard, we found a row of six small rooms (possibly 10 feet by 12 by 10), three above and three below, arranged as a wing to the main building. This wing is evidently a modern addition to the old house. It is built of wood; the thin walls are unplastered; there are no windows, but one door in each room, opening upon the court on the ground floor, and upon a narrow gallery above. A tiny fireplace with its chimney is the only ventilation when the door of a room is closed.

In these little rooms the heat was intense. In each one of these rooms we found an entire Italian family. . . . The toilet conveniences are the worst feature of this section; vaults are in fearful condition; 70 percent of them are bad. Of the 144 families, only 35 have separate vaults. The rest share water supply, yard, and toilet conveniences with their neighbors. . . . The floors in many of the tenements on the street level are wet and rotten. Not a single bathtub was found in the district visited.

. . . The streets surrounding the block are unpaved in part and appear never to have been cleaned—not within the memory of the present residents. The drainage is of the worst; gutters are cleaned once or twice a year.

. . . The average [family] income was found to be from $5 to $10 per week, 47.7 percent getting less than $5, and 76.7 percent getting less than $10.

The campaign against the Italians was part of a struggle involving primarily four factions of New Orleans' population. The first was made up of the old pre-Civil War commercial and professional elite, predominantly of Anglo-Saxon background, but also including people of French and Spanish stock, and joined since the Civil War by increasing numbers from the Irish and German populations. In the 1880s and 1890s this group organized the Reform Democrats. The second faction, supporting the Ring Democrats, was composed of the larger labor segments of these same ethnic groups, weighed more heavily toward the Irish, and containing some blacks. The third faction was the Italians, and the fourth the blacks.

The first faction, the anti-labor, anti-black anti-Italian elite of New Orleans, having succeeded in enlisting the white unions and many blacks in the repression of Italians, immediately turned on them to crush them also, the final phase of its divide-and-conquer policy.

In 1896, forty-six-year-old Walter C. Flower, one of the most powerful backers of Mayor Shakspeare, together with George Denegre, Walter Denegre, and John M. Parker, formed the "Citizen's Party." All four were leaders in the lynching of the Italians. Flower ran and was elected Mayor of the city. He defeated a labor-backed Ring candidate by cynically forming a very short-lived coalition, the Citizen's Party, of his own Reform Democrats, hated northern-oriented Republicans, angry populist whites, and blacks. A very wealthy man, a notorious enemy of labor, and two-time president of the powerful Cotton Exchange, Flower staffed his administration *entirely* from the Reform commercial aristocracy. He had been chairman of the Committee of Fifty during much of its persecution of Italians, having succeeded Edgar H. Farrar, who resigned the position four months before the lynching. With Flower's election, the city of New Orleans completed its overwhelming endorsement of lynching as a way of controlling ethnic minorities.

The labor unions, having joined in the oppression of Italians, and having taken over many of their jobs as a reward, were now pitted against blacks by Flower and the Reformers. As soon as the Italians were beaten, white laborers attacked blacks, and the next years saw race riots in the city. In March 1895, the Governor of Louisiana sent in the state militia to quell one of them which started when white dock workers attacked their black counterparts in a move to purge them from the waterfront. The use of troops effectively weakened both the white and black labor positions, and strengthened the commercial and professional class.

In the years right after the Italians' lynching, the rich commercial elite was enormously successful in its policy of crippling the white labor movement by keeping it preoccupied with hatred and fear of blacks. The Cotton, Sugar, Banking, and Rice Exchanges, run by the elite group, gained control of the state legislature as well as the city government, getting the votes of working-class and poor whites by patronage payoffs and by "nigger baiting." The dock business during this period multiplied fabulously. Most of the waterfront wealth went to the same Shakspeare-Flower group, while they kept labor in line by buying off "leaders" like James D. Houston, the lyncher of Italians who was rewarded by being made one of the controlling stockholders of a dock monopoly created by the city at the expense of Italian-Americans six weeks after the 1891 lynching. The monopoly so corrupted labor with do-nothing "patronage" jobs that historian George M. Reynolds reports that by 1920 "it was humorously said at the time that there were so many workers on the docks that it was impossible to get them out of the way so the ships could be loaded."

The Reformist and Ring effort against blacks must be seen in the light of the real political and economic power blacks had acquired in Louisiana during the Civil War and Reconstruction period from 1862 to 1877, hard for many Americans to appreciate today. Even before the Civil War, freed blacks had flocked to hurly-burly New Orleans because of the city's opportunities. In a

131

recent book, Benjamin Brawley reports that by 1860 one fifth of the taxable property in New Orleans belonged to "free persons of color." In another new study, Thomas Sowell explains:

> The large number of prosperous Negroes in New Orleans was due in large part of its having been a French [and Spanish] possession in which Negroes were treated according to the pattern prevailing in Latin-America rather than the pattern prevailing in the English-speaking colonies. One of the most prosperous New Orleans Negroes of the antebellum period left an estate of $100,000, and in 1894 another black man from the same city left an estate of nearly $500,000, even after a lifetime of philanthropy.

On July 30, 1866, a mob had attacked a white carpetbagger and black group attempting to hold a constitutional convention, killing 38 people and injuring 147—most of the casualties were black. But in 1868 the new constitution gave blacks the right to vote, on top of full equality (integration) given blacks in public schools and all means of transportation in 1867. Blacks used their ballot rights and in 1868 elected a black Lieutenant Governor named O. J. Dunn and twenty-nine black members of the legislature of Louisiana. In 1872, Lieutenant Governor P. B. S. Pinchback, a black, became Governor of the state when the incumbent was successfully impeached, and served from December 9, 1872, to January 13, 1873, and another black man, C. C. Antoine, became Lieutenant Governor that same year.

The next step after the riots of the mid-1890s in the campaign against blacks by the elite and its labor pawns was to take away their power by denying them the right to vote. Since the end of Reconstruction in 1875, the Reform and Ring groups, natural enemies except in their common persecution of blacks and Italians, had been slowly pushing the blacks out, while they concentrated on putting down the Italians. With the Italians beaten, a constitutional convention was called in Louisiana in 1898 to complete the process.

The convention adopted a new state constitution with a "grandfather clause," that is, it excluded from the right to vote any man who wasn't entitled to vote by law before 1867 and "his son or grandson." Of course, most Louisiana blacks weren't permitted to vote before 1867, and were disenfranchised by the clause. Whereas in 1898, 130,344 blacks were registered to vote in Louisiana, by 1900 only 5,320 were registered.

At the same time the racial integration of the entire South was canceled by the famous 1896 U. S. Supreme Court decision in *Plessy* v. *Ferguson* declaring racial segregation to be legal, a case which grew out of the suppression of blacks in Louisiana. In 1892, a man named Homer Adolph Plessy, who was "one-eighth Negro," had challenged an 1890 Louisiana law segregating the races on transportation facilities by refusing to leave a "White" railroad car and was arrested.

For good measure, the new 1898 constitution also effectively disenfranchised many Italian-Americans. It required five years of residence in the state, the ability to read and write the English language, and regular, frequent payments of a poll tax for all foreign-born people who registered after September 1, 1898. Many Italian-Americans in the city had not registered before this date because under the 1879 Louisiana constitution they were required legally to renounce their Italian citizenship in order to vote, and many of them cherished a hope, in vain for almost all of them, they they would someday return to Italy. In all, a large number of Italian-Americans were denied the right to vote by the 1898 constitution, exactly as the Reform members among its drafters had planned.

The Italians' right to vote was partly saved by the efforts of Ring Democrats at the convention, who by this time were at odds again with Flower's Reformers. Italian-Americans traditionally voted for Ring candidates, and the mayoral election of 1896 spurred many of them back to vote, or attempt to vote, in a vain try to keep former Committee of Fifty chairman Walter Flower out of office. The provision in the new constitution which protected the right to vote of some Italians was denounced on March 22, 1898, by the *Times-Democrat* because it would have permitted to vote "every illiterate white voter in Louisiana, every tramp, hobo and recently arrived Dago." The *Franklin News* agreed in a racist statement aimed at both blacks and Italians. The new constitution, it said, would make "the Dagoes citizens and disfranchise the Negro, and God knows if there is any difference between them it is largely in the darkies' favor."

Similarly, Italian-Americans had been attacked for organizing opposition to the attempt to take away their voting rights, and for trying to participate two years before in the mayoralty election which Flower won. The Washington *Post* had it both ways, accusing Italian-Americans of being indifferent to American customs and institutions, on one hand, and on the other of wanting to participate in the political process:

> The Germans, the Irish, and others . . . migrate to this country, adopt its customs, acquire its language, master its institutions, and identify themselves with its destiny. The Italians never. They remain isolated from the rest of any community in which they happen to dwell. They seldom learn to speak our tongue, they have no respect for our laws or our form of government, they are always foreigners. And now the Italian sojourners in New Orleans—excepting, of course, the few educated gentlemen of high social position, to whom none of these observations applies—are preparing for an excursion into local politics.

In a similar vein, the New Orleans *Times-Democrat* had affirmed the Italian-Americans' right to vote on March 24, 1896, but went on to say:

> when they interfere in American politics, and tell us what kind of a Constitution, what systems of law, and what suffrage is acceptable to them as Italians, they must arouse a very strong feeling against themselves and against those who would stir up these race prejudices, and organize the foreign-born population against the natives, in order to foster their own personal interest.

The persecution of Louisiana's Italian-Americans was hardly limited to political machinations. There were more lynchings of them in the state, at least two of them economically motivated according to historian Jean Scarpaci. In 1896, three Italian-Americans were lynched in Hahnville, Louisiana, three others in 1899 in Tallulah, Louisiana, and one in 1922. In addition, Italians were lynched elsewhere—in fact Italians were second only to blacks in numbers of lynch victims in the years 1870 to 1940. About 5,000 lynchings are on record in American history. About 1,200 of them were of whites, but most of these were before 1870. After that date, Italians were the only whites to join blacks as victims in any significant numbers. They were lynched in such states as Colorado, Mississippi, Illinois, North Carolina, and Florida.

The New Orleans Italian-Americans slowly overcame most of their suppression. The attempt to cripple Italian-American waterfront businessmen was resisted from the start by Macheca's sons and by other large Italian-American shipping companies, such as the Oteri Line and Pizzati Line, soon to be joined by the largest of all, the Vaccaro Line. Other Italian businesses—there were 3,000 of them in New Orleans in 1890—sprang back more slowly, as did the laborers, who were often employed by other Italians.

These efforts were hindered by the powerful image of Italians being responsible for New Orleans crime. The slur was not to be challenged until 1931. In that year the federal government's National Commission on Law Observance and Enforcement, known as the Wickersham Commission and made up of prestigious figures including the Dean of the Harvard Law School and a prominent New Orleans attorney named Monte M. Lemann, issued a report. The document's section on New Orleans contradicted the city establishment's efforts ever since Shakspeare and his phony list of ninety-four dago murders to smear the ethnic group. Page 339 of that section concluded:

> In so far as reliable evidence can be secured from police records, the foreign born in New Orleans play a very minor role in crime. This holds true whether consideration is given to the number of arrests made or the nature of the offenses. If the foreign born of any nationality are committing an undue portion of the crimes in the city, the police have not made available any evidence of it.

(Incidentally, the files of David Hennessy, and those of the New Orleans Police Department of his murder, were never made public. Some years ago when the time came for the department to turn over its records from the 1890s to the city archives, it delivered a near complete set, except for those of Hennessy and his murder. The department reported these had been "lost.")

The Wickersham Commission was even more to the point on page 342 of its section on crime and the foreign born:

> As a result of trouble with the Mafia in New Orleans between 1870–1890 which led to the lynching of 11 Italians charged with the murder of the chief of police in 1890, the general public is inclined to hold the Italians partly responsible for the city's high homicide rate. Since the Italians were charged with only four of the 543 homicides committed in New Orleans from 1925 to 1929, this feeling against the Italians seems hardly justifiable.

In its summary, the Commission concluded "it can be stated with considerable assurance that the foreign-born whites are the least criminal of the New Orleans population and the colored the most criminal with the native born standing somewhere between the two extremes."

The long fight upward against vicious obstacles for New Orleans' Italian-Americans passed more recent milestones. Their average income caught up with that of the city's other whites in the 1940s and '50s. Two mayors of Italian-American background were elected—Robert Maestri in the 1930s and Victor Schiro in the 1960s. This latter period also saw for the first time significant numbers of Italian-Americans being admitted to the politically, socially and economically very powerful top private clubs in New Orleans, including Shakspeare's own Pickwick Club, which elected a Sicilian American president in 1965. Some 15 percent of New Orleans' doctors, lawyers and architects are Italian-American today, as are some 10 percent of its judges.

The next decades after 1891 saw the triumph of the power of the commercial and professional elite in the state, as described by historian Leonard V. Huber:

During the post-Reconstruction years Louisiana politics had generally been controlled by the men who had been Civil War leaders and those of the upper classes such as bankers, lawyers, physicians, merchants, and business executives—in short, conservatives who decided who could run for office and who dictated policy after the candidates were elected. After 1900, when most of the Civil War crop of leaders had passed from the political scene, this group of conservatives still retained power, and together with the potent New Orleans politicians shaped the destinies of the state through their governors and legislators.

In the hands of the moneyed white elite, New Orleans' imports and exports increased from $133 million in 1900 to $593 million in 1929. Not only did the bulk of this wealth go to the small group making up the self-proclaimed "better class," but during that time this same class was to increase its ownership of land that produced the state's agricultural products—at the expense of ordinary farmers. Whereas 58 percent of Louisiana's farms were operated by exploited "tenant" farmers in 1900 (poor whites and blacks), by 1929, 66 percent of the state's land was worked by tenants for the state's wealthy faction.

The elite group made good use of the myths of David Hennessy's life and death in its accumulation of power. On May 29, 1892, the city of New Orleans dedicated a twenty-six-foot-high stone monument to him in lovely Metairie Cemetery. It took its place near the monument to Confederate General Stonewall Jackson erected in 1881, and the monument to the Louisiana Division of the Confederate Army erected in 1887, which shortly was to hold the remains of P. G. T. Beauregard upon his death in 1893. Funds for Hennessy's monument had been contributed from all over the United States, and included $430 from W. A. Pinkerton in Chicago. The inscription on the memorial reads: "His life was honorable and brave. His fidelity to duty was sealed with his death."

Two years later, a street in the city, which had been named for no less a personage than Napoleon, was renamed Hennessy Street.

The New Orleans lynching also fueled another political movement of exclusion, the anti-immigration nativist movement. "America for Americans" was the cry sweeping the country, the Washington *Post* reported three weeks after the lynching. "It is the almost universal belief," the paper continued, "that the next Congress will undertake to make some radical changes in the immigration laws." The nativists, led in Congress for thirty-one years until 1924 by the Italian-hating Henry Cabot Lodge, mutiplied their labors to see that this "universal belief" would be fulfilled. Their efforts succeeded in having Congress pass a literacy test in 1917, which was aimed mostly at Italians, for they were by far the group with the highest rate of illiteracy among the immigrants entering at that time, a rate that varied from year to year from 50 to 70 percent among the Italians landing. In 1921 and 1924, Congress then passed quota acts which, until 1968, cut off most immigration from all places except Protestant Northern Europe. The 1924 law limited Italian immigration to 3,845 per year whereas in the four previous years alone, despite the untold numbers of Italians excluded by the 1917 law, almost a half million Italians had entered the United States as immigrants.

The New Orleans affair gave birth to the American stereotype of Italian-Americans as criminals—that Italians started organized crime in the United States, that southern Italian culture is innately criminal, and that all or a substantial percentage of the people derived from that culture are somehow connected with crime. The result was the Italians suffered the most degraded image and worst treatment of all immigrants, as John Higham explicitly noted in his highly acclaimed 1967 book, *Strangers in the Land: Patterns of American Nativism*. He pointed out that:

> anti-foreign sentiment filtered through a specific ethnic stereotype when Italians were involved; for in American eyes they bore the mark of Cain. They suggested the Mafia, the deed of impassioned violence.

Higham cites typical examples, including the Baltimore *News'* old opinion that "the disposition to assassinate in revenge for a fancied wrong is a marked trait in the character of this impulsive and inexorable race."

Barbara Botein concluded a 1975 doctoral dissertation by saying:

> The Hennessy case also created a very negative and enduring image of Italian immigrants in the American mind. The very word "Sicilian" immediately evoked visions of half-civilized and hotheaded members of the Black Hand. This usually created a presumption of guilt whenever an Italian was charged with a crime. In the twentieth century, intellectual racists further downgraded the image of southern Italians by speculating that they were partly Negroid.

The last point of racism against Italian-Americans in our century is detailed in Barbara Miller Solomon's 1956 book, *Ancestors and Immigrants*.

The closest thing to an impartial investigation to the entire Hennessy case after that made by Federal District Attorney William Grant was conducted by John S. Kendall, albeit more than forty years later. He concluded that Monasterio, Antonio Marchesi, Polizzi, and Scaffidi were probably guilty, and that the other fifteen accused Italians were probably innocent.

Kendall's impartiality and thoroughness have been uncommon among commentators, most of whom do little more than repeat the allegations of the lynch leaders. One of the latest of these is David Leon Chandler, in his 1975 book *Brothers in Blood: The Rise of Criminal Brotherhoods*. This book is singled out not only because its author relies mostly on the lynchers' stories, taken on face value, without informing the reader of their source, but because Chandler elaborates on the stories, providing an excellent example not only of how myths, i.e., mixtures of truths and fancies, are perpetuated, but also how they grow. Adding to the lynchers' versions of events, Chandler also repeats as factual, without attributing their sources, the highly dubious self-serving accounts told by the Provenzanos at their second trial; the self-serving stories told by George Vandervoort, who profited enormously from the persecution of Italians; and Polizzi's wild confession, not permitted as evidence and never known except through secondhand versions told by policemen to reporters, including Polizzi's fantastic account that the Mantrangas were leaders of a group called the Stoppaglieri which was allegedly a rival of the Mafia. This story, as Chandler does not explain, also relies on an anonymous threatening note the Provenzanos introduced which they claimed was authored by the Mantrangas years before, complete with a hand-drawn crucifix, and which purports to be in the name of the Mafia, a curious thing for alleged rivals of the Mafia.

In his brief treatment of the Hennessy case, Chandler also presents some theories as accepted truth. For example, he writes that the Mafia got Thomas Devereaux appointed Chief of Detectives in 1881, an allegation not made by anyone at his appointment in 1881, or when Hennessy killed Devereaux that same year, or when Hennessy was killed nine years later. Not even Hennessy's staunchest praisers among the lynchers made such a claim, for it was well known that Devereaux was purely and simply a Ring hack. Chandler also says that Joseph P. Macheca "created" the "American Mafia."

In Chandler's book, material taken from the unidentified old accounts becomes a fascinating but fanciful tale, more sensational than those told by the lynchers themselves, or at any time since. For example, he implies that District Attorney Luzenberg and the judge at the Italians' murder trial aided Mantranga and Macheca, allegations never remotely suggested by Shakspeare and the lynchers, the real allies of Luzenberg and the judge. Thus, Chandler's account makes it seem that the Italians were acquitted with Luzenberg's connivance, and says that the judge sent them back to Parish Prison to protect them rather than probably to set them up for mob violence.

Chandler's only telling point to one who is familiar with these events is a psychological one. He claims that direct descendants of three of the nineteen Italians, Mantranga, Incardona, and Geraci, were named in 1972 (by whom he doesn't say) as members of the

"Louisiana Cosa Nostra family." If true, it does not prove anything about their ancestors' guilt or innocence in the Hennessy case. Nor do his references to Charles Mantranga's alleged life in organized crime long after he survived the lynching.

Interestingly, the New Orleans persecutors of Italians had formed the very type of organization they attributed to Italians with their alleged "vendetta societies" and Mafia. The behavior of the anti-Italians included secret meetings, terroristic violence used to gain and hold economic and political power, exclusion of "outsiders," appeals to honor and friendship, and justification of all this as a defense of their specific world and culture. And this "Italian" organizational style found expression in New Orleans with the formation of the White League just after the Civil War, before southern Italians came to the United States in significant numbers. Which ethnic groups learned what from whom?

These popular anti-Italian slanders continue very strong even in our own time of widespread sympathy toward other ethnic groups. As late as 1973, anti-Italian bigotry was expressed by a President of the United States. In the White House, Richard Nixon talked with his aide John Ehrlichman about rewarding groups in the American community that had voted for him in 1972—as did most of the country. The now famous Nixon tape recorders captured their conversation.

NIXON: The Italians. We mustn't forget the Italians. Must do something for them. The, ah, we forget them. They're not, we, ah, they're not like us. Difference is they smell different, they look different, act different. After all, you can't blame them. Oh no. Can't do that. They've never had the things we've had.

EHRLICHMAN: That's right.

NIXON: Of course, the trouble is . . . the trouble is, you can't find one that's honest.

Appendix A

Letter Sent by Mayor Shakspeare's Office to
C. H. Grosvenor of Athens, Ohio.

June 9, 1891

Honorable Charles H. Grosvenor
Athens, Ohio
Sir:—

Replying to your letter of May 29th, on the "subject of immigration especially with reference to Southern Italy, Sicily and etc.," I am directed by the Mayor to enclose you copies of:

I.—Report of the Committee of Fifty to the Mayor and Council on the events precedent to and following the assassination of Chief of Police Hennessy,

II.—A list forwarded to the Mayor by the Chief of Police Gaster of cases of murder and etc. committed by Italians and Sicilians.

On the subject of immigration the Mayor has to say generally that no part of our country is more inviting to immigrants than Louisiana, no people welcome honest new-comers more heartily, whether they come as capitalists or laborers. Our genial climate, the ease with which the necessaries of life can be obtained and the polyglot nature of the population unfortunately has singled this part of the country out for the idle and the emigrants from the worst classes of Europe, Southern Italians and Sicilians. New Orleans has an unusually large proportion of the immigrants from these countries [*sic*] and we find them the most idle, vicious and worthless people among us. A very large percentage are fugitives from justice or ex-convicts aided in their emigration by their government or the communities which seek relief by their departure. They rarely acquire homes, always band together, do not acquire our language and have neither respect for its government [*sic*] or obedience to its laws. They monopolize the fruit, oyster and fish trades and are nearly all peddlers, tinkers or cobblers (the two last trades are the ones taught in their prisons at home). They are filthy in their persons and homes and our epidemics nearly always break out in their quarter. They are without courage, honor, truth, pride, religion or any quality that goes to make the good citizen. New Orleans could well afford (if such a thing were lawful) to pay for their deportation. Except the Poles we know of no other nationality which is [as] objectional as a people. We think the immigration laws should be made as strict as possible and that citizenship or even domicile in this land should be held at the highest possible price, and safe-guarded by all means. The trouble about accepting certificates of further good conduct from Sicilians and Italians is that we would have little faith in the honesty of their issue and deem it best to absolutely exclude the people from both these countries [*sic*].

> I have the honor to be,
> Your obedient servant,
> [Signature illegible]
> Secretary.

Appendix B

Speech Made by Mayor Shakspeare to the City Council
on October 18, 1890

To the City Council: It is with the profoundest grief and indignation that I make to you the official announcement of the death of David C. Hennessy, superintendent of police of this city, grief at the loss of a true friend and an efficient officer—indignation that he should have died by the hands of despicable assassins. He was waylaid and riddled with bullets almost at his doorstep on last Wednesday night, and he died on Thursday morning at 9:06 o'clock.

The circumstances of the cowardly deed, the arrests made and the evidence collected by the police department, show beyond doubt that he was the victim of Sicilian vengeance, wreaked upon him as the chief representative of law and order in this community because he was seeking, by the power of our American law, to break up the fierce vendettas that have so often stained our streets with blood. Heretofore these scoundrels have confined their murderings among themselves.

None of them have ever been convicted because of the secrecy with which the crimes have been committed, and the impossibility of getting evidence from the people of their own race to convict. Bold, indeed, was the stroke aimed at their first American victim. A shining mark have they selected on which to write with the assassins's hand their contempt for the civilization of the new world.

We owe it to ourselves and to everything we hold sacred in this life to see to it that this blow is the last. We must teach these people a lesson that they will not forget for all time.

What the means are to reach this end I leave to the wisdom of the council to devise.

It is clear to me that the wretches who committed this foul deed are the mere hirelings and instruments of others higher and more powerful than they. These instigators are the men we must find at any cost.

For years past the existence of the stiletto societies among the Sicilians in this city has been asserted.

Appeal was made to me by a prominent Italian during my former administration to protect him from blackmail and murder, but as he was afraid to give any names I could do nothing for him.

It is believed that these horrid associations are patronized by some of the wealthy and powerful members of their own race in this city, and that they can point out who the leaders of these associations are.

No community can exist with murder societies in its midst. These societies must perish or the community itself must perish.

The Sicilian who comes here must become an American citizen, and subject his wrongs to the remedy of the law of the land, or else there must be no place for him on the American continent. This sentiment we must see realized at any cost—at any hazard.

The people look to you to take the initiative in this matter. Act! Act promptly without fear or favor.

Jos. A. Shakspeare, Mayor

Appendix C

The "Committee of Fifty" Appointed by Mayor Shakspeare

Edgar H. Farrar
(chairman until December
21, 1890)
Walter Flower
(chairman after
December 21, 1890)
Gen. Algernon S. Badger
Col. Thomas N. Boylan
Maurice J. Hart
John C. Wickliffe
George Denegre
Dr. D. H. Burns
E. J. Bobet
Thomas F. Agnew
Gen. John Glynn
Dr. C. Chassagniac
J. J. Keegan
Thomas Sully
Charles Garvey
Louis Arnauld
William B. Schmidt
Hugh McManus
C. Taylor Gauche
Clarence Fenner
William B. Ringrose
Prof. R. H. Jesse

Judge Robert C. Davey
G. H. McCartner
John N. Augustin
Louis Leonhard
John G. Byrd
James T. Hayden
John M. Coos
E. D. Soniat
Leonce Bouny
C. E. Schmidt
Charles R. Buck
William Redmond
Eugene May
A. J. Leverich
John Everett
C. Hanson
Joseph Garcia
Adolph Bartholomew
Ferd Claiborne
Henry Maspero
Joseph Voegttle
S. P. Walmsey
Col. James Lewis
A. A. Lelong
J. Lea McLean
John H. O'Connor

George W. Dupre
George A. Grandjean
Simon Hernsheim
W. W. Gordon
J. T. Witherspoon
B. F. Eshleman
George J. Burnes
Michael Foley
Peter S. Lawton
John Delaney
C. L. DeFuentes
James Richardson
Theodore Griffin
Jacob Hassinger
Marshall J. Smith
Dr. W. R. Mandeville
A. Valeton
B. C. Fisher

A. R. Broussard
John V. Moore
George F. Williams
Jules Aldige
James Legendre
Col. A. W. Crandell
Capt. Thomas O'Neill
John T. Gibbons
George F. Lord
E. Conery, Jr.
W. K. Wilson
Dr. George B. Lawrason
John M. Parker, Jr.
Charles Ballejo
John Holmes
T. J. Woodward
J. B. Sinnott

Appendix D

The Committee of Fifty's Open Letter to All Italian-Americans,
October 23, 1890

The committee of fifty appointed by the Mayor and Council to investigate the existence of stiletto societies in this city and to devise means to stamp them out has concluded for the present to act strictly within the limits of the law. We shall do everything in our power for the present to allay the popular excitement and to see that your people get full justice, and that no outrages are committed upon them. We believe that the great majority among you are honest, industrious, and good citizens, and abhor crimes as much as we do. These are the people to whom this appeal is directed. We want you to come forward and give us all the assistance and all the information in your power. Send us the names and history (so far as you know it) of every bad man, every criminal, and every suspected person of your race in the city or the vicinity. Whatever communications are made to us are strictly confidential. In giving this information, you may reveal your identity or not, just as you please. We would prefer that you should give your names and addresses in order that the committee may have personal communication with you. Address all communications to Lock Box No. 1,215.

We hope this appeal will be met by you in the same spirit in which we issue it, and that this community will not be driven to harsh and stringent methods outside of the law, which may involve the innocent and guilty alike. We believe this committee speaks the unanimous sentiment of the good people of New-Orleans when it declares that vendettas must cease and assassinations must stop. To this we intend to put an end, peaceably and lawfully if we can, violently and summarily if we must. Upon you and your willingness to give information depends which of these courses shall be pursued. We pledge the manhood of this community to protect and defend all those who come forward to assist and give us information.

Appendix E

The Nineteen Men Indicted for the Murder of David C. Hennessy

Pietro Monasterio Tried, no verdict reached. Lynched March 14, 1891.

Joseph P. Macheca Tried, found not guilty. Lynched March 14, 1891.

Antonio Marchesi Tried, found not guilty. Lynched March 14, 1891.

Gaspare Marchesi Tried, found not guilty. Set free after March 14, 1891.

Antonio Scaffidi Tried, no verdict reached. Lynched March 14, 1891.

Charles Mantranga Tried, found not guilty. Set free after March 14, 1891.

Emmanuele Polizzi Tried, no verdict reached. Lynched March 14, 1891.

Antonio Bagnetto Tried, found not guilty. Lynched March 14, 1891.

Bastian Incardona Tried, found not guilty. Set free after March 14, 1891.

James Caruso Not Tried. Lynched March 14, 1891.

Rocco Geraci Not Tried. Lynched March 14, 1891.

Frank Romero Not Tried. Lynched March 14, 1891.

Loretto Comitz Not Tried. Lynched March 14, 1891.

Charles Traina Not Tried. Lynched March 14, 1891.

Peter Natali Not tried. All charges dropped and set free after March 14, 1891.

Charles Pietza	Not tried. All charges dropped and set free after March 14, 1891.
Charles Patorno	Not tried. All charges dropped and set free after March 14, 1891.
Salvatore Sinceri	Not tried. All charges dropped and set free after March 14, 1891.
John Caruso	Not tried. All charges dropped and set free after March 14, 1891.

Appendix F

Members of the "Mantranga Group" Attacked on May 6, 1890

Anthony Mantranga
Vincent Caruso
Salvatore Sinceri
Rocco Geraci
Bastian Incardona
Antonio Lacascio

Appendix G

Those Arrested for the Attack on the "Mantranga Group" on May 6, 1890

George Provenzano	Not tried; charges dropped.
Peter Provenzano	Tried and convicted, July 18, 1890. Acquitted in second trial, January 23, 1891.
Joseph Provenzano	Tried and convicted, July 18, 1890. Acquitted in second trial, January 23, 1891.
Vincent Provenzano	Not tried; charges dropped.
Charles Patorno	Not tried; charges dropped.
Salvatore Giglio	Not tried; charges dropped.
Nicholas Giglio	Tried and convicted, July 18, 1890. Acquitted in second trial, January 23, 1891.
A. Pelligrini	Tried and convicted, July 18, 1890. Acquitted in second trial, January 23, 1891.
Anthony Impacaro	Not tried; charges dropped.
Peter Salvador	Not tried; charges dropped.
Gaspare Lombardo	Tried and convicted, July 18, 1890. Acquitted in second trial, January 23, 1891.
Anthony Gianfocarro	Not tried; charges dropped.

Appendix H

The Jury in the Trial of Nine Men for the Murder of David C. Hennessy

Jacob M. Seligman (jury foreman); jeweler
Arnold F. Willie; grocer
Henry L. Tronchet; clerk
William H. Leahy; machinist
Solomon J. Mayer; real estate
John Berry, Jr.; salesman
William Yochum; grocer
Charles Boessen; clerk
Walter D. Livaudais; railroad clerk
Edward J. Donegan; molder
William Mackesy; bookkeeper
Charles Heyob; clerk and piano tuner

Appendix I

Names Attached to the Newspaper Advertisement Calling
Together a Mass Meeting on March 14, 1891

John C. Wickliffe
Henry Dickson Bruns
C. E. Rogers
Samuel B. Merwin
L. E. Cenas
T. D. Mather
Septime Villere
W. P. Curtiss
C. E. Jones
John V. Moore
E. H. Pierson
E. T. Leche
W. S. Parkerson
J. G. Pepper
Richard S. Venables
Raymond Hayes
H. L. Favrot
Harris R. Lewis
Emile Dupre
Lee McMillan
T. S. Barton
D. R. Calder
Hugh W. Brown
Felix Couturie
J. C. Aby

J. G. Flower
W. Mosby
H. B. Ogden
Walter D. Denegre
A. E. Blackmar
S. P. Walmsley
C. J. Forstall
Thomas Henry
C. Harrison Parker
T. D. Wharton
Rud Hahse
James Clark
Charles M. Barnwell
Ulric Atkinson
George Denegre
C. L. Stegal
B. F. Glover
Wm. H. Deeves
F. E. Hawes
Omer Villere
John M. Parker, Jr.
James P. Mulvey
Wm. M. Railey
Charles J. Ranlett
J. F. Queeny

J. Moore Wilson

James Lea McLean

Edgar H. Farrar

Frank B. Hayne

C. A. Walscher

Thos. H. Kelley

H. R. Labouisse

A. Baldwin, Jr.

R. H. Hornbeck

Wm. T. Pierson

James D. Houston

Appendix J

Speech Made by William S. Parkerson to the Crowd at Clay Square on the Morning of March 14, 1891

People of New Orleans! Once before I stood before you for public duty. I now appear before you again, actuated by no desire for favor or prominence. Affairs have reached such a crisis that men living in an organized and civilized community, finding their laws fruitless and ineffective, are forced to protect themselves. When courts fail, the people must act! What protection, or assurance of protection, is there left us, when the very head of our police department, our chief of police, is assassinated in our very midst by the Mafia Society, and his assassins are again turned loose on the community? The time has come for the people of New Orleans to say whether they are going to stand for these outrages by organized bands of assassins, for the people to say whether they shall permit them to continue. I ask you to consider this fairly. Are you going to let it continue? Will every man here follow me, and see the murder of D. C. Hennessy vindicated? Are there men enough here to set aside the verdict of that infamous jury, every one of whom is a perjurer and scoundrel? Men and citizens of New Orleans, follow me, I will be your leader!

Appendix K

Letter from Consul Pasquale Corte to Ambassador Francesco Fava, March 15, 1891

New Orleans, March 15, 1891

Mr. Minister: I have not time to describe the horrors of the slaughter which the populace, under the leadership of the principal members of the vigilance committee, has committed against the unarmed prisoners, some of whom had been acquitted and some of whom had not yet been tried.

As early as the evening of the 13th instant the hisses and the stones thrown by the urchins in the street at the carriages in which the prisoners were gave ground for the apprehension that something serious would happen on the next day. The violent articles which appeared in the newspapers, such as the "Daily States" and the "Delta," which papers, in the name of the committee of fifty, announced that a meeting would be held on the following day to take vengeance, left no doubt as to the choice of the means of which it was proposed to make use.

It would have been sufficient, in the night, to change the lodging place of the prisoners in order not to expose them to certain death. Also, yesterday, when men armed with Winchester rifles began to collect at 9 o'clock in the morning, a word directing them to disperse would have been sufficient to prevent the butchery.

Hardly had the meeting commenced when I called in all haste at the city hall in a carriage, but neither the mayor nor his secretary was there, nor could anyone tell me where I could find him.

I found, however, in the mayor's room the attorney-general,

Mr. Rogers, and Mr. Villere, the deputy sheriff in charge of the prisoners, who told me they had come for the same purpose; but they appeared to me to be very calm and to be anticipating what was about to happen. I told the object of my visit, but they replied that they could do nothing without the mayor. I then made inquiries for Mr. Nicholls, the governor, and was told that he was not far away at a lawyer's office. I went there at once, and found him with the general in command of the troops and several other persons.

In view of the immediate danger for the prisoners and the colony, I requested him, in my official capacity as consul, to send troops or a guard of police to the place in order to prevent the massacre. He told me that he could do nothing until he was requested by the mayor. All that I could say was of no use. He asked me to sit down, saying that the mayor was at the Pickwick Club, and that he had telephoned to him to come at once. Twenty-five minutes elapsed, when the telephone announced that the mob was already at the prison doors, and that they had already hanged three of the prisoners. I went down and drove in my carriage at full speed to the prison, which was at a considerable distance. When I came near I saw a number of dead bodies hanged to trees; I saw that the massacre was over, and that the crowd was returning. I returned to the consulate, and at the door three colored men rushed at me, and, in order to keep them off, I was obliged to draw my revolver. A moment later Mr. Papini, clerk of the consulate, made his appearance, pale and greatly frightened, and told me that he had heard the crowd raise the cry of "Kill the Italian!" in consequence of which he had been obliged to take refuge in a store.

The crowd now started for Poydras Market, which is almost entirely inhabited by Italians. In the meantime the relatives of the victims and other Italians rushed to my office, desiring either to obtain the bodies through me or to seek advice as to the proper course to take. I told them to lock themselves up in their houses; and I went to the governor's office, in order to comply with the desire expressed by the relatives of the victims. I did not find him, but all that was asked for was obtained otherwise.

A number of low fellows came in the evening and pounded on the back doors of my house and violently pulled the front door bell of the consulate. They declined to give their names, but their intentions were manifestly hostile.

I inclose a copy of the letter which I have this day addressed to the governor, in pursuance of orders received by telegraph directly from his excellency the Marquis di Rudini.

I will thank you if, after reading this report, you will have the kindness to send it, with its inclosure, to the royal ministry, for which I offer you my thanks in advance.

Corte.

Appendix L

Mayor Shakspeare's Speech of May 16, 1891, to Italian-Americans Who Were Protesting the Expulsion of the Ethnic Group from All Businesses and Labor on the City's Waterfront

Joe Provenzano, I have sent for you to talk plain, straight English, and I mean every word I say to you. I and every other decent citizen am disgusted with the Dago disturbances and determined that they shall end immediately. Mr. Peters has told me that you threatened him, and I ordered him to swear out an affidavit against you. You need not deny it as your people deny everything, for we all well know that you are one of the leaders of a lawless, bloodthirsty gang.

You are now using the longshoremen as a means of recapturing the fruit landing. You have shown your hands and I call you down. The longshoremen have nothing to do with this business. They are not trying to cause trouble, and I have determined that any men in this city may work or quit when they choose, but no man shall be prevented from obtaining an honest livelihood if he will, and I do not mean to let you interfere with him or any one else. This is not the first time that the Provenzanos have made trouble, but it must and shall be the last. You have not learned the lesson taught your race by the people of New-Orleans, it seems, and I want you when you leave here to go home and tell your friends that if you make any more trouble, the police and Mayor of this city will not consider themselves responsible for the lives of you and yours. You need not tell me you are unjustly treated. You are constantly making trouble, and a Mantranga cannot pass a Provenzano in the street without being shot at. You and your tribe are after revenge on the Mantrangas. The fruit business is the proof of it, and I tell you it must stop.

I am not afraid to talk to you like this, because I am not afraid of you or the Italians. I leave the city to-day. In my absence I have instructed my representatives and the police to keep a watch on you, and when I return I will act for myself. I intend to put an end to these infernal Dago disturbances, even if it proves necessary to wipe every one of you from the face of the earth.

Appendix M

Report of the Grand Jury Which Investigated the Lynchings

Grand Jury Room, May 5, 1891

To the Hon. Robert H. Marr, Judge of Criminal District Court of the Parish of Orleans, Section A.

When this Grand Jury entered upon its term of service there was pending in Section B, this tribunal, the trial of nine men, indicted for participation in the assassination of the late superintendent of Police, D. C. Hennessy, on the night of Oct. 15, 1890.

The enormity of that crime, executed at the midnight hour, created unusual interest throughout the whole country, while in our own city, vitally concerned in the administration of justice as deeply affecting her social, political and material welfare, the sentiment of the populace had crystallized into a concrete form of expression that justice be rendered through the recognized channels of criminal jurisprudence, that the guilty perpetrators, whoever they were, be tried by an impartial jury of American citizens, and meet with a righteous conviction. One fact stood out in awful prominence, above and beyond dispute or question by any man— the fact that a crime of unparalleled atrocity had been committed, evidenced by the five terrible death-dealing weapons, the numerous slugs and bullets fired on their errand of human destruction and found imbedded in the fences and houses at the scene, besides the missiles that struck down the solitary man, who would never have been marked as the victim had he not filled the responsible position of chief officer of the law.

It is not to be wondered that attention should be directed to the trial during the many days of its progress in the selection of jurors, the evidence of witnesses, the arguments of counsel, and the charge of the Judge, and that it should be finally concentrated on the twelve men who by virtue of their solemn oaths, sat in awful judgment on their fellow-men. The verdict is now of official record, bearing date March 13, 1891. We cannot be mistaken in the assertion that the verdict was startling, amazing, a bitter disappointment, shocking to public opinion, provoking the repeated accusation that some of the jury had been unfaithful to their office. We feel that we do not transcend the limits of our duty as the grand inquest to refer to the strong presentation of the case as made the State through counsel associated in the prosecution. Clear, continuous, complete, convincing in the direct testimony and the material circumstances, it appeared more than sufficient to convince the most unwilling listener with its truth and convey the full measure of its power to those who ventured a doubt.

As the trial neared its termination it was not possible for any observer to fail to realize the tenor of the comments made on every side touching the action of some members of the jury when the case should be submitted. Charges and speculation abounded, coupled with the well-known connection of certain parties of unenviable notoriety as shown by their presence daily in the court-room and building, arousing the suspicion that the most subtle, dangerous, and powerful influence known to the practice of criminal law was being exercised in behalf of the defense. These considerations have led us to investigate the subject embracing all its attendant conditions and incidents. The inquiry has been conducted with the utmost diligence, devoid of fear or partiality, with the single purpose of fastening the guilt on the proper persons and presenting them under indictment to this tribunal.

Each one of the twelve jurors of the trial was summoned and asked to make a statement. None objected, but all rather welcomed the opportunity. It was a notable feature of the sworn statements that they primarily sought to justify their verdict by attacking the line of evidence presented by the State and attaching much weight to the arguments of counsel for defense. It was freely admitted by the jurors that remarks had been made in the jury room as early as the first day when testimony was offered, and repeated a number of times afterward, "that the State was making a poor case," and the remark was positively repeated at the close of the State's evidence. One quarrel, at least, was reported, arising from the accusation by one juror to another with the expression, "You talk like you were fixed before you came here." They formed no conception of the tension to which the public mind was strung, though impressed with the deep interest as shown each day by the crowd of spectators in the courtroom.

It was clearly indicated that the necessity for secrecy was urged, as the several jurors were selected and joined the company of their fellows. It was impressed upon them at various times, and finally, before the verdict was rendered, brought forward again, with the injunction to destroy every vestige of evidence they had and leave every thought and act behind them. Surely the urgency of this was most cunningly devised to conceal the peculiar events that transpired in the jury room. Careful observers testify with special reference to the marked inattention of the jury as the witnesses submitted their evidence—a conduct most unbecoming and fraught with the gravest consequences when the momentous import of the issue is considered. We are led to conclude that the jury undertook to try the case when it was submitted by their own estimate of the value of statements made by parties not called as witnesses. With strange unanimity they dwelt upon what they knew by reading and hearsay of certain incidents of the assassination prior to the trial, and made these the basis of the powerful persuasion for giving the accused the benefit of the doubt and concluding the deliberations in their favor.

We must take occasion to say that it was not expected to obtain any evidence of undue influence from the members of the jury, for those who were uncorrupted had nothing to reveal, while the others would not make themselves particeps criminis, yet in their numerous statements much was obtained having a direct connection with and supported by the great volume of testimony elicited during the course of the inquiry.

It is clearly brought out by evidence of the jurors that as affecting three of the accused, Politz [*sic*], Scaffidi and Monasterio, the jury engaged in the deliberations in their case some four or five hours, attended with intense excitement, and on repeated ballots the jury's vote stood six guilty, six not guilty. This is a clearly defined indication of the convictions of the jury as to the three accused. It impressed us deeply, as it must every one to whom the fact is conveyed, and forces the conclusion that the evidence was sufficient to justify the six jurors who stood resolute and determined for a verdict of guilty, making it well-nigh impossible to reach any other conclusion than a mistrial. These three accused, named above, were probably the unwilling actors designated by leaders of the conspiracy to execute a villainous part in which they had neither personal motive nor interest.

Following this investigation, it was quickly learned from various sources that talesmen had been approached. Every clue offered was taken up; as a rule, the talesmen who had been previously marked out were seen when alone or invited away to some secluded and unsuspected place, well designed pretexts guarding the real meaning of the talks, but quickly leading up to the great trial. Talesmen were visited at their houses during the evening or early morning, intercepted while on their way to the Court House, stopped in the corridor of the court, and the vile work was deliberately carried forward in the courtroom during the trial. One favorite expression was that "big money might be made by going on the jury and doing right." There is no possible doubt that such attempts were made by various parties in the service of the defense —entertained by some of the talesmen and scornfully rejected by others. These are facts given on the evidence of talesmen, who, quickly discerning the true meaning of the men who addressed them, indignantly replied to any attempt to control their line of conduct by these emissaries. In several instances a rebuff was answered that the talk was a joke, but surely a well-directed joke of deep significance, when the leading part is enacted by the counsel of one of the accused participants in the assassination at the time awaiting trial in the Parish Prison now under indictment for attempting to bribe a juror.

Another class of the talesmen took special care to deny any knowledge of the vile work or showed remarkable deficiency of memory as to what they had told their friends, causing us to conclude that they were silent from fear or had been seen and cautioned about incriminating any one, till their tongues were silenced as with the hand of death. In this connection we can plainly state that a number of the witnesses most emphatically denied having been approached or spoken to about service on the jury, even after telling it to their friends, who had informed us. Yes, there were young men from whom better things were expected. Of such we can say that to conceal, and thereby attempt to condone a crime is only a step removed from participation in it.

Among the talesmen, a number of our citizens have nobly come forward from a sense of duty, resisting their experiences, furnishing at least some of the missing links in the chain of circumstantial evidence drawn around the organized gang of jury bribers. It is not to be questioned that the work was systematically executed after careful preparation, and it had to be done quickly, as the hours were few and time precious. The Grand Jury knows that the list of 500 talesmen in the Hennessy case was in the office of O'Malley & Adams at 11 o'clock Sunday morning, Feb. 22, 1891, though the trial Judge issued special orders Saturday evening that the list was not to be made public or given to counsel of either side until Monday morning. It is not shown by whose hands the list was secured, but enough is shown to confirm the past secret and powerful influence of the so-called private detective agency and Counselor Adams to handle the machinery of the court.

The official relations of the Jury Commissioners to the court in the trial of criminal cases are so intimate and far-reaching in their consequences that the maladministration of their duties has become the fountain source of the successful fixing of jurors in important trials. Great or small pieces of evidence show that the lists of names were tampered with when drawn from the jury wheel and before they reached the jury box in the court. O'Malley was put in possession of the lists almost immediately after the names were drawn and before they reached the District Attorney's office in due course. Influential friends alone could accomplish these ends, but it was secured in the person of one of the Commissioners lately removed. It is further shown that in the office of this detective agency is kept a book of names and addresses of jurymen, out of 300 names drawn for the February panel, 32 were on the list in O'Malley & Adams's office, and later, as the talesmen were drawn, many more names appeared that were on that private list. At times special lists were brought to the Jury Commissioners, which one of them stated had been prepared elsewhere, and being looked over by the others, went into the jury wheel. Truly, the business of this enterprising detective agency was facilitated, when 32 names of their selection could be drawn on a panel of 300 jurors from a wheel containing 1,000 names.

We must express regret that any cause should exist for the criticisms directed toward some of the Deputy Sheriffs employed in the court and at the Parish Prison. Unreliability seems to be the feature marking their conduct, interrupting the confidence which should clothe every subordinate officer of the law. There were those whose indifference was so manifest—while not detected in any act of infidelity—that suspicion was aroused as to their sympathy with the accused, calculated to embarrass the best-directed efforts of the prosecution. It is a noteworthy point in this connection that the indictments against McCrystol and Cooney being read in the courtroom in blank, the fact was at once communicated to them through some of the subordinates of the court. Under a proper condition of things the utmost secrecy should have been observed. It is further shown that when the arrest was made of these two parties in the office of O'Malley & Adams the Deputy Sheriff was asked by O'Malley to say the arrest was made on Carondelet Street, and it was so reported to the court.

In searching for the true causes of the criminal actions connected with the empaneling of the jury in the Hennessy case the sworn statement of Thomas C. Collins is found of great value, and in this place we take occasion to declare that Collins was selected especially for the duties to be performed, and for this purpose secured employment in O'Malley & Adams's office, which, being done, he was commissioned a special officer by the Mayor and paid by the city for this service. The money received by him each week from O'Malley & Adams for services rendered there was handed to the designated person at the City Hall. The difficult and dangerous duties assumed by Special Officer Collins, while acting in his double capacity, were performed with strictest fidelity, as is evidenced by the daily reports in writing of everything seen or heard. They are minute in all details, their correctness is assured; in fact, the material features of the statement and reports are so closely connected and interwoven with the facts and circumstances connected with the trial, as confirmed by various other witnesses, that there is not the slightest reason to doubt their accuracy and correctness. They unfold the whole story of the iniquitous workings of the arch conspirator and his lieutenants, revealing the boundless power of a man to overcome and defy the majesty of the law on criminal and civil proceedings through the operations of an unscrupulous private detective agency. Truly may it be said that the greater the freedom of action and the removal of restraint under the liberal privileges accorded all men in our country the bolder becomes the unlawful practices, the greater the villainy, of such a combination of designing and unscrupulous malefactors.

It is well known to the court, and will be quickly realized by every thoughtful person that the difficulties of establishing the existence of a conspiracy by adequate proof are almost insurmountable. Such plottings are done in secret places and their workings often guarded by the advice of counsel well versed in criminal law. Secrecy is an essential element in the successful execution of the designs of a conspiracy. Seldom does it happen that any one of the participants will reveal the villainy either before or after its execution.

In the attempts to influence the talesmen of the Hennessy case no visible act was committed, and we fully realize the difference between a crime committed by words only and what are known as visible acts, which might be witnessed by other persons who could tell the tale of crime. In the attempts to influence talesmen, and the successful part of it, whispered words conveyed the insinuation or directly offered the money influences. This reference will serve to show the barriers this inquest has encountered in securing evidence, but sufficient was offered by voluntary and reliable witnesses to justify the indictment of six men as follows:

Thomas McCrystol and John Cooney, with D. C. O'Malley, for attempting to bribe a talesman, and Bernard Claudi, Charles Granger, and Ferneard Armant, for attempt by each to bribe three different talesmen. These parties are closely shown to have been intimate with O'Malley, often at his office, informed of all doings, and were active workers in the jury-fixing business generally.

We are prompted to express ourselves in deprecation of the hesitation of many of our citizens to be connected with criminal prosecution by seeking relief from jury duty. The intelligent and law-abiding, with those engaged in the various enterprises of business and trade, must recognize the obligation, without which the guilty too often go unpunished. We urge them to cast off this repugnance to rise superior to the annoyances attendant upon trials, standing up with the great majority of their fellow-men in the condemnation of the detestable practices brought to a high degree of perfection by the frequency of their practices, which threaten to deaden and destroy the virtues of the Criminal Code, to debase the temple of justice to ignoble ends, and degrade the cherished right of "trial of jury" from its high position as the exponent of truth, justice and right.

Taking into account the volume of testimony admitted by the numerous witnesses before this Grand Jury, and considering that evidence not only in the abstract relation to each party, but to its aggregate and collective bearing, we are forced to the conclusion that Dominick C. O'Malley is chargeable with a knowledge of and participation in most, if not all, of the unlawful acts in connection with that celebrated case. With his skill, as acquired by years of experience, the most cunningly-devised schemes were planned and executed for defeating the legitimate course of justice, the chief aim and object being to place unworthy men upon the jury in the trial of the nine accused. Without the assiduous and corrupting influence, we believe the verdict would have been radically different, and as a natural consequence the tragic occurrences of the 14th of March last never would have been recorded.

In the persons of the indicted McCrystol and Cooney there were reliable and trained assistants; the former's connection with some intermissions extended back through several years. McCrystol's voluntary statement to the Grand Jury, partly in the shape of a confession, reveals some points of the trial and causes us to think he would have told more but for the power and influence of O'Malley and his associates. We know that such influence has been used in connection with a friend of the nine men lately on trial. The two men were the trusted accomplices, and figure throughout the whole affair with a prominence showing the high appreciation in which their services were held. They are the men who approached several talesmen, as before stated, the proposals being mostly refused. In one instance it is shown that O'Malley took money from his safe and gave it to Cooney, who said: "McCrystol, you know that fellow better than I do; give him the money." This was to complete a bargain reported made with a talesman who was shortly after accepted as a juror. And here mark the words of one Fanning: "You fellows better get up there now."

We cannot fail to refer to the intimate relations existing between a class of ward politicians and the prime mover in all the infamous doings; his office was a place of rendezvous; all were deeply concerned in the appointment of a successor to the late chief, and speculation abounded as to the availability of such a one for their use. It was also important that the agency should be informed of the workings of the city special officers, and O'Malley managed to have a friend appointed. He was assigned to the police and not the detective force, when he resigned rather than wear a uniform.

We have it most directly and confirmed by other evidence that a person holding a position of Inspector of Weights and Measures was often at the agency and stood sentinel at the door several times. This same person was seen coming to the Court House in

171

company with a talesman the day he was accepted as a juror. There is confirmed evidence that the influence of D. C. O'Malley with the night watchman and inspector at the electric light plant was so great that he could cause them to manipulate the light at the corner of Girod and Basin streets the evening the jury was taken to the scene of the assassination. We quote the words of Officer Collins showing the directions by O'Malley at the detective agency. 7 P.M., March 10: "Go to Mike Fanning's and, if he is not at home, to the Electric Light Company and see Jim Waldron and tell him I sent you. Tell Waldron in a manner no one but he will be able to understand, to make that light at the corner of Girod and Basin burn weak as it was on the night of Oct. 15; to have it done by 7:20 o'clock."

The message was delivered to Waldron, and on the messenger's return O'Malley remarked: "That fellow will break that wheel down if necessary." No wonder, then, O'Malley had access to the electric light works after nightfall and it doubtless accounts for the alteration found in one of the record books as to the condition of the light at the corner of Basin and Girod streets on the night Hennessy was shot, it being changed to read forty minutes additional of dim light to the time originally recorded, for the fatal night of Oct. 15, 1890. It is but justice to state that the President and Superintendent of the Electric Light Company, as also the General Manager, who was in New York, so soon as they were informed that their men were being tampered with did all and everything in their power to frustrate their plans and preserve the actual record.

From the beginning of our investigation, there is continuous evidence brought to our attention of the pernicious combinations of what is known as the D. C. O'Malley Detective Agency. It advertises in the *Daily City Item* and by a sign board at the office that one of the ablest criminal lawyers at the bar is the attorney for the agency. We know for an absolute fact that the bank account is kept and checks drawn in the name of O'Malley & Adams, the interested parties being D. C. O'Malley and Lionel Adams. Such a combination between a detective and a prominent criminal lawyer was unheard of before in the civilized world, and when we contemplate its possibilities for evil we stand aghast.

The indictment of D. C. O'Malley for perjury was based upon most undoubted evidence that he came originally from Cleveland, Ohio, where on Jan. 30, 1878, he was convicted of petty larceny and committed to the workhouse of the city of Cleveland, where he served a term expiring June 22, 1878. He next appears under indictment for perjury in the United States Circuit Court at New Orleans, where an indictment was based upon the affidavit against one Ed Schleider, which O'Malley afterward contradicted under oath, but he managed to secure an acquittal, owing to the timely disappearance of the affidavit, which he alone was interested in having suppressed. Later he was committed to the Parish Prison for attempting to levy blackmail upon one George W. Randolph in the proceedings against Randolph for interdiction. The following record is verified by officials, showing his numerous offenses before the criminal court of this parish.

1. No. 9,478, July 3, 1884. Indicted for attempting to prevent witnesses from appearing and testifying. Nolle prosequied April 26, 1884.

2. No. 4,838, May 9, 1884. Indicted for threatening and intimidating a witness, acquitted May 29, 1884.

3. No. 2,262, June 3, 1879. Pleaded guilty to carrying concealed weapon and sentenced.

4. No. 3,679, Nov. 3, 1883. Convicted of assault and sentenced.

5. No. 930, April 1, 1881. Pleaded guilty to carrying a concealed weapon and sentenced.

6. No. 3,678, Jan. 3, 1883. Pleaded guilty to carrying a concealed weapon and sentenced.

7. No. 5,186. Pleaded guilty to carrying a concealed weapon and sentenced.

8. No. 7,242, Dec. 4, 1885. Convicted of carrying a concealed weapon and sentenced.

9. No. 7,241, May 22, 1885. Indicted for assault and battery.

So pernicious to the administration of justice were his doings and methods found, that while Judge Roman presided in the criminal court, he ordered that O'Malley be excluded from the court room. This was during the time his present associate, Lionel Adams, was District Attorney, and it is a significant fact that the two indictments against O'Malley for tampering with witnesses were not brought to trial but were nolle prossed by the District Attorney just prior to the expiration of his term.

The inside view which we are enabled to get of the workings of this agency through City Detective Collins, abundantly corroborated from many sources, convinced us that it had at its command a board of perjurers, blackmailers, suborners, and jury tamperers, and that it has for some time been an element of discord in this community and a stumbling block to the administration of justice which should be eradicated. That its career of crime has not been cut short is a matter of wonder, and is no doubt due to the fact that O'Malley and his co-workers have banded together for self-preservation. The evidence is beyond question that O'Malley went up town in the Carondelet street car on Saturday, 14th March last, in company with a party reaching Fourth Street shortly before 11 A.M. The party was sent twice to Seligman's house, after which O'Malley in person went to the house, and within a few minutes Seligman was running up Carondelet Street and entered a carriage in waiting near the corner of St. Charles and Washington avenues. O'Malley was next seen walking rapidly up St. Charles Avenue. Were it possible for any doubts to exist as to the acquaintance and sympathy, or even closer bond of fellowship existing between these two men, it must be dispelled by the above recital, as showing the first thought and effort for Seligman when O'Malley realized the danger expressed in the thundering tones of popular indignation.

The extended range of our researches has developed the existence of the secret organization styled "Mafia." The evidence comes from several sources fully competent in themselves to attest its truth, while the fact is supported by the long record of blood-curdling crimes, it being almost impossible to discover the perpetrators or secure witnesses. As if to guard against exposure, the

174

dagger or stilletto is selected as the deadly weapon to plunge into the breast or back of the victim and silently do its fearful work. Revenge was their motto. Jealousy and malice speedily found solace in these methods, while the burning vengeance of the vendetta sought satisfaction in the life blood of an enemy.

Officers of the Mafia and many of its members are now known. Among them are men born in this city of Italian origin, using their power for the basest purposes, be it said to their eternal disgrace. The larger number of the society is composed of Italians and Sicilians, who left their native land, in most instances under assumed names, to avoid conviction and punishment for crimes there committed and others were escaped convicts and bandits outlawed in their own land, seeking the city of New-Orleans for the congenial companionship of their own class. These men knew the swift retribution of the law in Italy for hundreds have been shot down at sight by the military in the mountains of Sicily without a second thought. To-day there is recorded in the office of the Italian Consul in this city the names of some 1,100 Italians and Sicilians landed here during several years past, showing the official records of their criminality in Italy and Sicily. Hundreds of them are among us to-day. We doubt not the Italian Government would rather be rid of them than be charged with their custody and punishment.

Such is the well-known character of a part of the Italian colony, as it is called, who are domiciled in this city and its vicinity. It cannot be questioned that secret organizations whose teachings are hostile to the fundamental principles of the Government of the United States must be a continual menace to the good order of society and the material welfare of the people. Whether the name be Mafia, Socialist, Nationalist, or whatever it may be, whether situated in New-Orleans, Chicago, or New-York, the meetings of their members create and disseminate seditious opinion, with a manifest tendency toward overt acts whose commission partakes of the rankest treason.

We may say that the many societies created and chartered for the laudable purpose of exercising a healthful influence in the various departments of the body politic enjoy a hearty approbation and are productive of good results. But in marked contrast to all those is the Mafia, whose every thought and act is in opposition to law and order as contemplated by every nation of the civilized world and in open defiance of the statutes of this state and Nation and the cherished traditions of the people. Law is truly regarded as the embodiment of the wisdom of all ages, and its just execution the safeguard of society by the punishment of transgressors; its just execution expresses the will of the people in condemnation of crime, but where this lofty principle is condemned by the practice of assassination for revenge or spite, and concealment under the most binding oaths renders powerless the efforts of the law to reach the chief actors and to secure witnesses, it becomes the duty of the people in the exercise of their sovereign rights to issue their decree of condemnation. That verdict has been rendered. The power of the Mafia is broken. It must be destroyed as an element of danger, a creation of leprous growth in this community.

Taking into account the mass of evidence presented, which is only partially summarized in the foregoing, it becomes our painful duty to make a declaration most severe in its reflection upon the action of some of the jurymen. We are so deeply impressed with the facts of the case that the moral conviction is forced upon us that some of the jurors impaneled to try the accused on the charge of assassination of the late Chief of Police were subject to a money influence to control their decision. Further than this, we may say it appears certain that at least three, if not more, of that jury were so unduly and unlawfully controlled. Some of the jurors themselves have testified in most emphatic terms that if it had not been for the persistent and well-directed efforts of three of the jurymen, most conspicuous from the time that body was impaneled, the verdict would have been materially different from that rendered. This is a sad and terrible commentary from their associates on the jury, as against those whose every action was intended to make them the controlling power. It is certain that the special effort of counsel for defense was to select for service on that jury such men as were of the acquaintance and well under the influence of O'Malley and his assistants, notably those talesmen who were on the detective agent's list.

What can be thought when three of the jurors were accepted with only some unimportant question, or the clerk told to "swear" them without a question! This is a proceeding almost unheard of in trials for capital offenses, but it has its meaning, as well as the other instances have their significance. One of the jurors young in years was, by his own statement, so susceptible to the influence of a dream that he changed his mind between night and morning. Others of the jury plainly stated that their age and inexperience did not qualify them to assume the responsibilities of jurymen. In that case, impatience prevailed toward the close, and it is thought by several of the jurors to have hastened the conclusion. Surely a remarkable jury, but fully competent to render the remarkable verdict. It has gone to the people whose intelligence and virtue enable them to discern between truth and falsehood, to decide between right and wrong.

No question is more intimately connected with the subject matter of this report than that of immigration. It deeply interests the people of this whole country by reason of the good results following the landing on our shores of large numbers of meritorious and law-abiding foreigners, or the damage attendant upon the introduction of a vicious or indolent class who leave their native country for that country's good, seeking as asylum here, soon again to follow in their footsteps of the past. We know that this question more deeply concerns the city of New-Orleans than it does any city on the Atlantic seaboard. The great importance is forcibly expressed in the columns of the public press till there seems to be an awakening to the danger that threatens us in the situation and to the necessity for a radical reformation. That past immigration laws were sadly deficient or badly administered is indicated by recent legislation of the National Congress, and even these new regulations will not be effective unless strictly enforced by the proper officials charged with such duties. That is the intention at present and for the future, yet by some design or other the details of the law may be evaded. For instance, so high an authority as the Italian Consul, this city, in his sworn statement before the Grand Jury charged that nine Italians were recently landed from the steamship Entella whose names were not on the passenger list. This point has been referred by him to the Italian Government and is being investigated, the steamer being due at Palermo about this time. The Consul claims that 941 persons were landed, while the passenger register showed 932 names. If it is actually shown that these nine Italians were so landed, in violation of the laws of both nations, they should be returned whence they came and the steamship Entella heavily fined.

We have stated in our remarks about the Mafia that several hundred Italian criminals are in this city to-day who should not have left their native land without the indorsement of the American Consul as to character, and should not have been permitted to land here. The time has passed when this country can be made the dumping ground for the worthless and depraved of every nation. The crisis is reached, and on the magnitude of the issue it becomes the duty of the next Congress to quickly enact such vigorous laws that complete protection be afforded henceforth against these evils.

At the same time we shall plainly say from our own experience and knowledge that a large part of the Italian colony in this city is recognized as a worthy class. They do not indulge freely in the use of beer or alcoholic drinks, are fairly industrious, and those who remain in the city soon save up a few dollars, more by the strictest frugality than otherwise, and soon are doing something for their own account. As if by common consent, the fruit and oyster business has drifted into the hands of the Italians, the volume of which in wholesale and retail lines reaches immense proportions. What more do they want! What more could they ask! No other country in this earth would extend to any newcomers such privileges. And what do we ask in return! Simply that they, like all others of foreign birth, should conform to existing laws by which their persons and property are protected, assimilate in thought and deed with our people in denouncing the wrong and upholding the right, rise above the fears and persuasions of secret societies, helping to crush their power, and above all else, showing an allegiance to the principles of the national and State Governments with no doubtful fidelity, realizing that the one flag, as the emblem of freedom, not less than the index of a nation's power, is the Stars and Stripes, which must and shall be respected. It may be thought we have exceeded the bounds that should compass the report of a Grand Jury, but let it be remembered that the subjects embraced are of such extraordinary character in connection with the events of the recent past that to some extent we are compelled to refer to them from our position as citizens as well as from our present official relations to this honorable court.

In the presentation of the main features given to us as evidence, condensed as far as possible by the selection of the most important portions of the inquiry, we have referred mainly to the evidence bearing upon the trial of the nine accused in Section "B" of this honorable court but directly connected with all those circumstances are the terrible events transpiring on the 14th day of March last—events which in themselves may be charged as directly traceable to the miscarriage of justice as developed in the verdict rendered on March 13. We are deeply impressed with the serious charge delivered by your Honor to this body on the subject, and at no time since have we lost sight of the necessity for a thorough investigation of all the conditions antecedent to it. We have engaged ourselves most assiduously with the examination of a large number of witnesses, embracing those who were present at the meeting on Canal Street, in the vicinity of the Parish Prison, as well as several hundred of our fellow-citizens taken from every rank and class of society.

It is shown in the evidence that the gathering on Saturday morning, March 14, embraced several thousands of the first, best and even the most law-abiding, of the citizens of this city, assembled as is the right of American citizens, to discuss in public meeting questions of grave import. We find a general sentiment among these witnesses, and also in our intercourse with the people, that the verdict as rendered by the jury was contrary to the law and the evidence, and secured mainly through the designing and unscrupulous agents employed for the special purpose of defeating the ends of justice. At that meeting the determination was shown that the people would not submit to the surrender of their rights into the hands of midnight assassins and their powerful allies.

The assassination of the late Chief of Police shows the culmination of a conspiracy. His death was deemed necessary to prevent the exposure and punishment of criminals whose guilt was being fast established by his diligent pursuit. The condition of affairs in this community as to a certain class of violators of the law had reached such a state that the law itself was well-nigh powerless to deal with them, so far-reaching was their power and influence in the trial of criminal cases. Good citizens were profoundly impressed by the repeated and signal failures of justice. The arts of the perjurer and briber seemed to dominate in the courts, paralyzing and rendering powerless the ends of justice. Certainly this was a desperate situation. In the public meeting above referred to —general and spontaneous in character as truly indicating an uprising of the masses—we doubt if any power at the command of the authorities would have been sufficient to overcome its intentions. Evidence is before us from official resources that eleven persons were killed in the attack on the Parish Prison. In the careful examination as to citizenship of these men, we find that eight of them were beyond question American citizens and another had "declared his intention" in this court, which act carries with it the renunciation of allegiance to his native country.

It is a noteworthy fact in connection with the uprising that no injury whatever was done to either persons or property beyond the one act which seemed to have been the object of the assemblage at the Parish Prison. We have referred to the large number of citizens participating in this demonstration, estimated by judges at from 6,000 to 8,000, regarded as a spontaneous uprising of the people. The magnitude of this affair makes it a difficult task to fix the guilt upon any number of the participants—in fact, the act seemed to involve the entire people of the parish and city of

New-Orleans, so profuse is their sympathy and extended their connection with the affair.

In view of these considerations the thorough examination of the subject has failed to disclose the necessary facts to justify this Grand Jury in presenting indictments.

Appendix N

*Consul Corte's Open Letter to the Grand Jury
Denouncing Its Report*

May 6, 1891

W. H. Chaffe, Esq., Foreman of Grand Jury, City:

Sir—I am surprised to see printed in the report of your honorable body, published in the papers to-day, a great alteration of certain parts of my statements made not only before you, but especially of those made to Mr. Lafaye and another member of the grand jury at my residence and not under oath of secrecy.

If, as it is publicly asserted, some members of the grand jury were in the mob and that body is trying to excuse their actions, it does not concern me personally, but I cannot allow my statements to be altered or partially published with the object of drawing inferences contrary to my deductions.

It is my opinion that solidity should exist between good elements in order to guard against bad ones and in this sense asked by the above two gentlemen if there are any Italian criminals in this city, I did not hesitate to reply, without giving the number, that there are not a few, as there are of other nationalities, but I added that it would be difficult to get rid of them either because the most of them are naturalized Americans who have the support of politicians and certain authorities or either because extraditions were so costly in the United States.

I cited as an instance the extradition of Esposito, to which most of the American press expressed itself in opposition, and which was successful at a heavy expense, and because the demand to extradite was made in the Northern States.

182

Just because there are a great number of criminals here, I was surprised to see persons sacrificed whose precedents were good and who were acquitted or not yet tried.

As to the incident on the Entella referred to in the report of the grand jury, I was asked by Mr. Lafaye on the 1st instant if what was published in the *Delta* on the 29th ultimo was true; but as I had just returned here from Pensacola I replied that I did not know to what he alluded. Having read the article I saw that by a mistake it referred to the steamer Elysia, of the Anchor Line, and then I said that as to the Entella I was surprised that the parties delegated expressly by the Mayor to examine into the condition of the immigrants did not notice that 841 passengers landed, while the list called for only 832. This explains plainly to me how easily fugitives from justice could be introduced in this country if authorities incompetent in office or in such matters were entrusted with said investigations.

And it is partly to this undue mingling of outsiders in the temple of justice that I ascribe the bloody tragedy.

But the agreeable silence, the studied reticence and other accompanying irregularities will never destroy the truth of the acts occurred and which I denounced to my government, viz.: That an extra judicial body appointed by the Mayor from the beginning premeditated, as it appeared in its appeal, the killing of the prisoners; that the same body assembled on the night of the 13th of March to take, in cold blood, the necessary steps to kill, for political purposes, defenseless but fearful adversaries; that about twenty parties, among them some representing the law and order, executed said project, preventing before the commission of the deed the admittance in prison of the large crowd of children, women and others, gathered through curiosity; that innocent Italian blood was shed; that not only nothing was done by the authorities to prevent it, but a few officials contributed directly or indirectly in order to accomplish the work, and finally, that the names of the participants in the killing, as well as those of the instigators, are of public notoriety. Respectfully,

P. Corte, Consul of Italy

Appendix O

Mayor Shakspeare's Letter to Governor Nicholls, May 16, 1891

To His Excellency,

   Francis T. Nicholls,

      Governor of Louisiana.

Governor:–

Under date of May 6th, 1891, the Consul of Italy at this port, Mr. P. Corte, saw fit to address to W. H. Chaffe, Foreman of the Grand Jury, then in session, a very remarkable letter. The evening of the day in which it was written, the Consul sent copies of the letter by the hands of his Secretary to the daily papers for publication. I enclose a printed copy of that letter.

Your Excellency, being resident in New Orleans, is fully aware of the fact that ever since the assassination of Superintendent of Police Hennessy, on October 15th, 1890, the papers have teemed with all manner of vaporings from Mr. P. Corte in the shape of interviews etc. For these reported sayings he could not properly be held as an official responsible, and since he was scarcely credited with one statement before another was made either exactly the opposite of or largely qualifying the first, his vagaries and blusterings were regarded by all but his own people as either laughable or contemptible. This letter of May 6th, however, to the Foreman of the Grand Jury is over his official signature, "P. Corte, Consul of Italy," and must be noticed. It has been noticed by the Grand Jury and very properly returned by that body to the writer as being impertinent. Besides being impertinent, the letter contains statements absolutely false and beyond question known to be false by Mr. Corte.

If as Italian Consul, Mr. Corte has ever had any usefulness here, he has outlived it and has become through his own acts not only an unacceptable person, but an element of danger to this community, in that by his utterances, he incites his inflammable people to riot or sullen opposition to the laws and customs of a country they have sought as an asylum. Being the depository, as he confesses himself to be, of criminal secrets relating to the individuals of his race resident among us, he refuses to give to the departments of police and justice the information he has, and thereby increases the danger to the community from these criminals.

For these reasons I have the honor to request that you ask of the Honorable Secretary of State at Washington, the recall of Consul Corte's Exequartor by the President. This application would have been made to you sooner, but for the reason that I desired to place in your hands to accompany your note to the Secretary of State, a report made to the Mayor and Council by the "Committee of Fifty." I enclose a copy and beg to call your Excellency's attention to that part of it relating to Mr. Corte.

I have the honor to be,

Your obedient servant,
Joseph A. Shakspeare
Mayor of New Orleans.

Appendix P

*Report by Federal District Attorney William Grant to
U. S. Attorney General William H. H. Miller*

New Orleans, La., April 27, 1891

Sir: In compliance with the directions contained in your letters of March 25 and 30, I beg to inform you that I have made a thorough investigation as to the nativity and citizenship of the alleged Italian subjects who were killed in the parish prison on the 14th of March last. I now submit the result of my examination on these points, together with a general but brief statement of the circumstances which preceded this unfortunate occurrence.

These persons were indicted, with others, on the 13th day of December, 1890, in the criminal district court of the State, No. 14414 on the docket, for the alleged murder of David C. Hennessy on the night of October 15, 1890: Antonio Scaffidi, Antonio Bagnetto, Antonio Marchesi, Pietro Monasterio, Charles Traina, Manuel Politz [Polizzi], and Loretto Comitz as principals, and James Caruso, Rocco Geraci, Frank Romero, and Joseph P. Macheca as accessories before the fact.

At the same time another indictment was found against them for the same offense and filed under the No. 14415. Copies of both are annexed to this report, marked Exhibits Nos. 1 and 2. They were arraigned and pleaded not guilty to both indictments.

About the middle of February last they were arraigned for trial on indictment No. 14414 before section B of said criminal court, Judge Baker presiding, whereupon the State obtained an order of severance and proceeded with the trial of nine only of the accused, among them six of those subsequently killed.

186

Of these Bagnetto, Marchesi, and Macheca were found not guilty on the 13th day of March, 1891, and as to Scaffidi, Politz, and Monasterio, there was a mistrial, the jury failing to agree.

The verdict was rendered about 12 o'clock, and some time during the night of that day a meeting was held by certain persons who were dissatisfied with the verdict, which resulted in a call for the populace to assemble at Clay statue, on Canal Street, at 10:30 o'clock A.M. the next day, to take into consideration the vindication of the law on account of the failure of the jury to convict. The next morning at the appointed hour a large crowd assembled at Clay statue, and from there proceeded to the parish prison, where the accused were confined, and, forcing an entrance, shot them to death. Of the eleven killed, Antonio Bagnetto, Antonio Marchesi, and Joseph P. Macheca had been tried and acquitted, and Antonio Scaffidi, Manuel Politz, and Pietro Monasterio had been tried, but the jury disagreed and there was no verdict. The others, James Caruso, Loretto Comitz, Frank Romero, and Rocco Geraci, had not been tried.

I now proceed to give in detail a history of each person killed, so far as I can from the evidence I have been able to obtain.

Antonio Scaffidi made his declaration before the criminal district court for the parish of Orleans for the purpose of becoming a citizen of the United States October 10, 1887, stating that he was 22 years old, born in Italy, arrived in the city of New York March 5, 1880 (see Exhibit 3); registered as a voter in Orleans Parish, La., on said declaration October 3, 1890 (see Exhibit A); indicted for the murder of Hennessy December 13, 1890; tried, but jury failed to agree on a verdict. The Italian consul states that he was born in Brolo, province of Messini, from whence he came to the United States, when about 14 years of age, under a passport dated November 19, 1880. (According to his own statement in his declaration, he arrived in New York October 5, 1880.)

Antonio Bagnetto made declaration before the criminal district court for the parish of Orleans for the purpose of becoming a citizen of the United States August 29, 1887, stating that he was a native of Italy, 41 years old, arrived in New Orleans December,

1875 (see Exhibit 4); registered as a voter in Orleans Parish, La., December 26, 1887 (see Exhibit A); indicted for the murder of Hennessy December 13, 1890; acquitted March 13, 1891. The Italian consul states that he was born in Palermo, and came from there to New Orleans in 1875; that he was a sailor, and that his true name was Antonio Abagnatto. His book of record, which all Italian sailors must have, and which is a substitute for a passport, is deposited at the consulate. The consul gives him a good character.

James Caruso made declaration before the criminal district court September 18, 1886, for the purpose of becoming a citizen of the United States, stating that he was a native of Italy, 32 years old; arrived in New Orleans March 8, 1867 (see Exhibit 5); registered as a voter in Orleans Parish, La., September 18, 1886 (see Exhibit A). This man always took part in politics and voted. He was at one time a commissioner of elections in the Fifth ward (see affidavits of John Journee, George Provenzano, Paul Ducastaing, and Joseph Provenzano). Indicted December 13, 1890, for the murder of Hennessy, but not tried. The Italian consul states that his true name was Gerolamo Caruso, and that he came from Palermo when so young as not to need a passport. (As he came to this country in 1867, and was 32 years old in 1886, when he made his declaration, he must have been about 13 years old when he arrived.)

Antonio Marchesi made declaration of intention to become a citizen of the United States before the criminal district court of Orleans Parish October 3, 1890 (see Exhibit 6); registered as a voter October 3, 1890, in Orleans Parish (see Exhibit A); does not appear to have taken an active part in politics nor to have voted. The Italian consul states that his true name was Antonio Grimando, and that he came to New Orleans from Roccamena, province of Palermo, under a passport dated October 10, 1888, and that he is supposed to have had some trouble with a woman, not resulting, however, before he came to this country, in his being charged with any crime. His passport is deposited at the consulate. The records of the custom-house show that he arrived in New Orleans November 19, 1888, per steamship *Plata*, from Palermo, under the name of Antonio Grimando. He was indicted for the murder of Hennessy December 13, 1890, and acquitted March 13, 1891.

Manuel Politz made declaration to become a citizen of the United States before the criminal district court of Orleans Parish October 13, 1890, stating that he was a native of Italy, 29 years old; arrived in New Orleans December 25, 1884 (see Exhibit 7); registered as a voter in Orleans Parish October 13, 1890 (see Exhibit A). He signs himself Emanuelle Polizzi in his declaration and on the registration rolls, but it is evidently the same name. Indicted December 13, 1890, for the murder of Hennessy; tried, but the jury failed to agree, and there was a mistrial March 13, 1891. The Italian consul states that he was born in San Cipriano Jato, Italy, and that his name was Emanuelle Polizzi; that he came to New Orleans in 1882, and is reported to have been an unruly character in Italy, although he was never tried for a crime. His passport, if he had one, had not been deposited at the consulate. At one time he lived in Austin, Tex., where he cut a man with a knife.

Joseph P. Macheca, born in New Orleans in 1843; occupation, merchant; residence 206 St. Claud street, New Orleans; registered as a native of Louisiana and as a voter October 6, 1886 (see Exhibit A); voted and took an active part in politics (see affidavits of John Journee and H. R. Ducastaing); indicted December 13, 1890, for the murder of Hennessy, and tried and acquitted by the jury March 13, 1891. He is admitted by the Italian consul to have been an American citizen.

Frank Romero obtained final papers of naturalization April 4, 1868, before the fourth district court of Orleans Parish as a citizen of the United States (see Exhibit 10); registered as a voter April 3, 1888, in New Orleans (see Exhibit A); voted and took an active part in politics (see affidavits of George Provenzano and John Journee); indicted December 13, 1890, for the murder of Hennessy, but not tried. He is admitted by the Italian consul to have become an American citizen by naturalization.

Rocco Geraci. The Italian consul states that he was born in Monreale, near Palermo, Italy; that he was registered as a voter in this city in 1880, as appears from a certificate of the registrar deposited in the consular office some time ago, but lately sent to the Italian minister in Washington; that he was charged with murder in Italy, but escaped to this country in 1878 before he could be arrested, but was condemned in contumacy and sentenced to ten years' imprisonment. The depositions of George and Joseph Provenzano, John Journee, Dan Douglass, and Mike Early, herewith transmitted, show that he took an active part in politics and voted at elections. He must have made a declaration of his intention to become a citizen before he could receive a certificate of registration. Thus far I am unable to find the record of his declaration or registration. He had no passport.

Charles Traina does not appear to have taken any steps to become a citizen, nor to have taken part in politics, nor voted, under this or any other name. The Italian consul states that his true name was Vincenzo Traina; that he was born in Contessa, Entallina, Italy, and came to New Orleans under a passport dated October 17, 1882, at the age of 30. His passport is deposited at the consular office. He was indicted for the murder of Hennessy December 13, 1890, but not tried. For two years prior to the assassination he was a laborer on Sarpi plantation, and it is said he came to New Orleans the day before Hennessy was killed and returned the day after.

Loretto Comitz; occupation, tinsmith; residence, 192 South Liberty street, New Orleans; does not appear to have made any declaration of intention to become a citizen of the United States, nor to have registered as a voter in this city. He was indicted for the murder of Hennessy December 13, 1890, but never put on trial. The Italian consul states that he was born in Neevella, near Rome, where he was convicted on a charge of theft and sentenced to three years' imprisonment. He came to this country some twenty years ago, but whether he escaped or left Italy after serving his time does not appear. If he came under a passport, it is not deposited at the consulate.

Pietro Monasterio arrived in New Orleans January 7, 1890 per Italian steamship *Plata,* and is described on the passenger list as a shoemaker by occupation, 46 years old, from Palermo (see certificate of collector of the port, marked Exhibit 8); indicted for murder of Hennessy, December 13, 1890, but there was a mistrial March 13, 1891. The Italian consul states that he came from Caccamo, Italy, where he had a wife and five children, and gives him a good character. His passport is deposited in the consular office.

From the foregoing history of each of the persons killed it will be seen that Joseph P. Macheca was a native of Louisiana and Frank Romero was a fully naturalized citizen, having taken out his final papers and voted; that Antonio Bagnetto, Antonio Scaffidi, Rocco Geraci, and James Caruso had made the preliminary declaration of their intention to become citizens of the United States and had registered as voters and voted in the parish of Orleans; that Manuel Politz and Antonio Marchesi had made their preliminary declarations and registered as voters, but that Charles Traina, Loretto Comitz, and Pietro Monasterio had made no declaration of their intentions to become citizens and had not voted or taken part in politics, as far as known.

As to the alleged bribery of the jury which tried the persons accused of the murder of Hennessy, I have to report that my examination does not connect any of the persons killed with that charge, if true.

Some indictments have been lately found against D. C. O'Malley, a detective employed in the defense, charging him with an attempt to bribe talesmen summoned on the jury, and an inquest is now being held, and it is understood that the grand jury have found true bills against other persons on the same charge; but the evidence on which the grand jury acted is not accessible to me.

I am unable to obtain any direct evidence connecting these persons with the Mafia, or any other association of a similar character in the city. The existence of such a society has been known and believed in by the public generally for a great many years, but its secrets have never been penetrated by the civil authorities. Few of those living who have been its victims have the courage to speak. Of the many persons whom I have examined on the subject, only two, George and Joseph Provenzano, have been willing to disclose the truth in an affidavit. They have testified to the existence of the society and furnished evidence of its practices in the form of blackmailing and threatening letters, which I forward attached to their affidavits. In this connection, I forward a statement made by the chief of police of this city, showing a great number of murders, affrays, and assaults committed by Italians in this city during the last twenty-five years, the perpetrators of which have not been punished, because the evidence was suppressed or concealed. I do not draw the inference myself from the facts disclosed by this statement that these crimes were all the work of the Mafia, but they are attributed to that society generally by the public.

I have not attempted to examine into the guilt or innocence of the persons accused of the murder of Hennessy. The evidence in the case against them submitted to the jury is voluminous, covering some 800 pages of typewriting. Both as a whole and in detail it is exceedingly unsatisfactory, and is not, to my mind, conclusive one way or the other. I have endeavored to ascertain whether they have been lawabiding citizens since their arrival in this country, but have not been able to connect them with any criminal practices prior to their indictment in the Hennessy case, except in the case of Manuel Politz, who is reported to have assaulted and cut a person in Austin, Tex., some years ago.

As to their history before they came to this country, I have taken the statement of his excellency the Italian consul at this port, and the information is noted below each name. From this it appears that Rocco Geraci and Loretto Comitz were escaped criminals when they came to the United States.

I have received a communication from his excellency Pascale Corte, Italian consul, relating to the civil status of the alleged Italian subjects at the time they were killed, which I have the honor to forward herewith for your consideration. He claims that even if these persons had made a declaration of their intention to become citizens of the United States, and afterwards exercised the right to vote given by article 185 of the constitution of the State of Louisiana, still they are not to be considered citizens until they have resided in the United States for a period of five years and have been granted final papers, as provided by section 2165 of the Revised Statutes of the United States.

Without presuming to give an opinion on this question, which, I assume, is to be dealt with by the political department of the Government, I take the liberty of suggesting that after these persons renounced allegiance to their King, and while maintaining their residence in the United States and exercising the privilege of citizens, they ought to be held to have renounced all claim to the protection of the country of their nativity.

Respectfully submitted.

William Grant,
United States Attorney.

Bibliography

Articles

Aaronson, R. R. "A Piece of Bread," *Common Ground*, Vol. 7 (Autumn 1946), pp. 22–26.

———. "The Pecan Tree," *Common Ground*, Vol. 10 (1949), pp. 75–88.

Brandfon, Robert L. "The End of Immigration to the Cotton Fields," *Mississippi Valley Historical Review*, Vol. 50 (1964), pp. 591–610.

Bryce, James B. "Legal and Constitutional Aspects of the Lynching at New Orleans," *The Living Age*, Vol. 189 (June 6, 1891), pp. 579–85.

Carr, John F. "The Coming of the Italians," *The Outlook*, Vol. 82 (1906), pp. 418–31.

Corte, Pasquale. "La Colonia Italiana negli Stati del Texas, Mississippi, Florida, Alabama, Arkansas, e Luigiana," *Bollettino del Ministero degli Affari Esteri*, 1891 (Italian Government), pp. 9–14.

Coxe, John E. "The New Orleans Mafia Incident," *Louisiana Historical Quarterly*, Vol. 20 (1937), pp. 1067–1110.

Cunningham, George E. "The Italian: A Hindrance to White Solidarity in Louisiana," *Journal of Negro History*, Vol. 50 (1965), pp. 22–36.

"Exterminating the Mafia," *Illustrated American*, Vol. 6 (Supplement to March 28, 1891), pp. 1–15.

Hackney, Sheldon. "Southern Violence," *American Historical Review*, Vol. 74 (1969), pp. 906–25.

Karlin, J. Alexander. "New Orleans Lynchings in 1891 and the American Press," *Louisiana Historical Quarterly*, Vol. 24 (1941), pp. 187–204.

———. "Notes and Documents: The Italo-American Incident of 1891 and the Road to Reunion," *Journal of Southern History*, Vol. 8 (May 1942), pp. 242–46.

———. "Some Repercussions of the New Orleans Mafia Incident of 1891," *Research Studies of the State College of Washington*, Vol. 11 (December 1943), pp. 267–82.

Kendall, John S. "Who Killa de Chief?" *Louisiana Historical Quarterly*, Vol. 22 (1939), pp. 492–530.

Lodge, Henry Cabot. "Lynch Law and Unrestricted Immigration," *North American Review*, Vol. 152 (1891), pp. 602–12.

"The Mafia and What Led to the Lynching," *Harper's Weekly*, Vol. 35 (March 28, 1891), pp. 225–27.

"Mafia Execution Role in N.O. Told," New Orleans *Times-Picayune*, June 19, 1955.

Mario, Jessie White (Vedova). "Italy and the United States," *The Nineteenth Century*, May 1891, pp. 701–18.

Marr, Robert H. "The New Orleans Mafia Case," *American Law Review*, Vol. 25 (1891), pp. 414–31.

McMain, Eleanor. "Behind the Yellow Fever in Little Palermo: Housing Conditions Which New Orleans Should Shake Itself Free From," *Charities and the Commons*, Vol. 15 (November 4, 1905), pp. 152–59.

Moroni, Giacomo. "L'Emigrazione Italiana Distretto Consolare di Nuova Orleans," *Bollettino dell' Emigrazione*, 1910 (Italian Government), pp. 17–25.

"New Orleans' War on the Mafia," *Illustrated American*, Vol. 6 (April 4, 1891), pp. 319–23.

Persico, Joseph E. "Vendetta in New Orleans," *American Heritage*, Vol. 24 (June 1973), pp. 65–72.

White, Melvin J. "Populism in Louisiana during the Nineties," *Mississippi Valley Historical Review*, Vol. 6 (1918), pp. 7–10.

Books

Asbury, Herbert. *The French Quarter: An Informal History of the New Orleans Underworld.* New York: Alfred A. Knopf, 1936.

Biographical and Historical Memoirs of Louisiana. 2 vols.; Chicago: The Goodspeed Publishing Company, 1892.

Brawley, Benjamin, A. *Social History of the American Negro.* London: Collier-Macmillan, 1970.

Chandler, David Leon. *Brothers In Blood: The Rise of the Criminal Brotherhoods.* New York: E. P. Dutton and Co., 1975.

Crotty, William J. (ed.). *Assassinations and the Political Order.* New York: Harper & Row, 1971.

Fortier, Alcée. *A History of Louisiana,* Vol. IV. New York: Manzi, Joyand & Co., 1904.

Higham, John. *Strangers in the Land: Patterns of American Nativism.* New York, 1967.

Hobsbawn, E. J. *Primitive Rebels*. New York: W. W. Norton & Co., 1959.

Horan, James D., and Howard Swiggett. *The Pinkerton Story*. New York: G. P. Putnam's Sons, 1951.

Huber, Leonard V. *New Orleans: A Pictorial History*. New York: Crown Publishers, 1971.

————. *Louisiana: A Pictorial History*. New York: Charles Scribner's Sons, 1975.

Jackson, Joy J. *New Orleans in the Gilded Age: Politics and Urban Progress, 1880–1896*. Baton Rouge: Louisiana State University Press, 1969.

Kendall, John S. *History of New Orleans*, Vol. II. Chicago and New York: The Lewis Publishing Co., 1922.

King, Moses, and M. F. Sweetser. *King's Handbook of the United States*. Buffalo, N.Y.: Moses King Corporation, 1891.

Landry, Stuart Omer. *The Battle of Liberty Place: The Overthrow of Carpet-Bag Rule in New Orleans, Sept. 14, 1874*.

Louisiana: A Guide to the State. Writers' Program of the Works Projects Administration. New York: Hastings House, 1945.

New Orleans City Guide. Federal Writers' Project of the Works Progress Administration. Boston: Houghton Mifflin Company, 1938.

Prezzolini, Giuseppe. *I Trapiantati*. Milan: Longanesi & C., 1958.

Reynolds, George M. *Machine Politics in New Orleans*. New York: Columbia University Press, 1936.

Schiavo, Giovanni. *The Truth about the Mafia and Organized Crime in America*. The Vigo Press, 1962.

Shugg, Roger W. *Origins of the Class Struggle in Louisiana*. New York: 1953.

Smith, Dwight C., Jr. *The Mafia Mystique*. New York: Basic Books, 1975.

Solomon, Barbara Miller. *Ancestors and Immigrants: A Changing New England Tradition*. Cambridge, Mass.: Harvard University Press, 1956.

Sowell, Thomas. *Race and Economics*. New York: David McKay Co., 1975.

Sprout, Harold, and Margaret Sprout. *The Rise of American Naval Power, 1776–1918*. Princeton, N.J.: Princeton University Press, 1939.

Thirty Years of Lynching in the U.S., 1889–1918. New York: NAACP, Arno Press, 1969.

Tylen, Alice Felt. *The Foreign Policy of James G. Blaine*. Minneapolis: University of Minnesota Press, 1927.

Volwiler, Albert T. (ed.). *The Correspondence Between Benjamin Harrison and James G. Blaine, 1882–1893.* Philadelphia: The American Philosophical Society, 1940.

Woodward, C. Vann. *The Strange Career of Jim Crow.* New York: Oxford, 1966.

Documents and Records

Records of the Criminal Court of New Orleans, Book ⅍10, Dec. 1890–1892.

Records and Correspondence of the Office of the Mayor of New Orleans. Archives, New Orleans Public Library.

New Orleans Police Department Illustrated. Police Mutual Benefit Association, 1900.

Congressional Record, Fifty-second Congress, First Session, Vol. 23.

Foreign Relations of the United States, 1891, and *1892.* Washington, D.C.: U. S. Department of State, 1892, 1893.

File ⅍11914-90, General Department Files, Department of Justice. National Archives, Washington, D.C.

File ⅍7896 Adjutant General's Office, War Department Archives. National Archives, Washington, D.C.

Annual Reports of the Secretary of the Navy, 1889 to 1892. Washington, D.C.: Government Printing Office.

Unpublished Theses and Dissertations

Adams, Margaret. "Mafia Riots in New Orleans." M.A. Thesis, Tulane University, 1924.

Botein, Barbara. "The Hennessy Case: An Episode in American Nativism, 1890." Ph.D. Dissertation, New York University, 1975.

Carroll, Ralph Edward. "The Mafia in New Orleans," M.A. Thesis, Notre Dame Seminary, New Orleans, June 1956.

Carroll, Richard Lewis. "The Impact of David C. Hennessy on New Orleans Society and the Consequence of the Assassination of Hennessy." M.A. Thesis, Notre Dame Seminary, New Orleans, June 1957.

Iorizzo, Luciano J. "Italian Migration and the Impact of the Padrone System." Ph.D. Dissertation, Syracuse University, 1966.

Karlin, J. Alexander. "The Italo-American Incident of 1891." Ph.D. Dissertation, University of Minnesota, 1940.

Robert, Mary Elizabeth Phillips. "The Background of Negro Disenfranchisement in Louisiana." M.A. Thesis, Tulane University, 1932.

Scarpaci, Jean Ann. "Italian Immigrants in Louisiana's Sugar Parishes: Recruitment, Labor Conditions and Community Relations, 1880–1910." Ph.D. Dissertation, Rutgers University, 1973.

Newspapers

The following newspapers on and about the dates cited in the pages of this book:

New Orleans *Daily Democrat*.

New Orleans *Daily Times*.

New Orleans *Times-Democrat*.

New Orleans *Daily Picayune*.

New Orleans *Daily Item*.

New Orleans *Mascot*.

New Orleans *Daily States*.

New Orleans *New Delta*.

New Orleans *Lantern*.

New York *Times*.